LEGACY OF
ENGAGEMENT

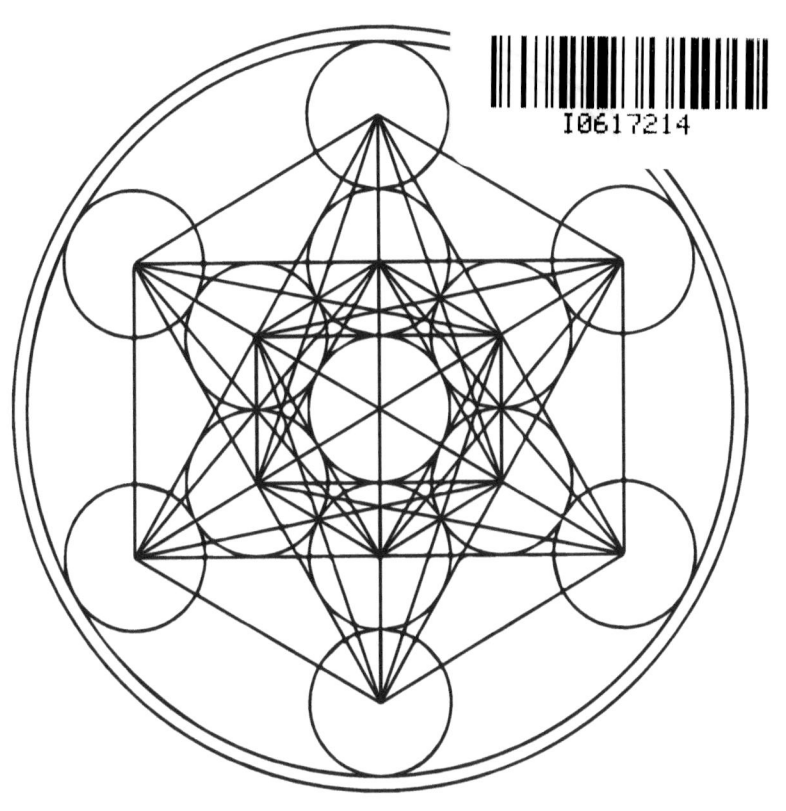

I0617214

Ricky Nieuwenhuis
and
Lindi Masters

Contents

Chapter 1
Echo Chamber Of Light

We're entering into an era and into a season where the words we speak and how we engage heart to heart is going to transform our lives. There has to be a result in what we do. We don't have conferences, teachings and books just for the sake of it. We are beginning to engage and behold the secrets of Yahweh for us as sons in our day.

A while ago Yahweh laid it on my heart to write the Legacy series. I remember waking up early one morning to behold some things and Yahweh spoke very clearly to me about administrating some processes we have gone through as sons within the Kingdom Realms and to bring them down to a place where people can behold, engage, trade and see the mystery of what is unfolding in their lives personally.

Trading has transformed my life. I get surprised when I hear people still trying to figure out the importance of trading. We are at a place where we shouldn't question our trade. It should come from something that happens within our hearts because we want to behold what has been released within the atmosphere. When I engage with a teaching, I am fully aware of the life and journey of those who are speaking. They are not just speaking words but are beholding the transformation and the fruit they see in their lives and are echoing their lives into the atmosphere. This becomes our portion when we listen to them and position our heart correctly.

So, when I listen to a teaching, I don't have it playing in

the background and hope to hear something that I like. I sit, listen, engage and behold, so when something happens within my heart because a statement is declared and a shift happens within the arena that I operate from, I immediately make a mental note of an amount I need to trade and I hold that within the chambers of my mountain. I either release it immediately or I behold and sit on it in case something else comes from the same place and I arc with it and an amount begins to accumulate as I engage. I begin to trade into that individual's life because I want what they have.

I am where I am (and I'm still going to places) that supersedes my expectation and even my desire because I trade and put value on the person's life and I put value on their encounters, the sacrifices, the places they have had to navigate as sons to begin to behold a message that they then have to confine to an hour-long teaching. When we put value on that it will transform us.

One of the key things within this journey of sonship within the Legacy series is the maturity that is unfolding within my life. This has come from me recognising who I am. That sounds like a glib statement but there is more to it than that. The moment we recognise who we are everything begins to change. If we do not recognise who we are and if we do not understand what we carry, then I personally believe we will never be able to fulfil our testimony scroll. If we are still wondering if we're mature enough for this and if we've gone through a process for decades but still do not see the fruit, we start thinking about what we should and shouldn't have done and we lose focus of the truth of why we are here. We are here for a purpose – to bring about a transformation to creation. This all happens when we understand who we are, where we are positioned, and when we operate from that Kingdom into creation there's a transformation that has to be expected. I don't believe that the church at large understands who they are and that's the reason we do not see transformation taking place within creation.

Christianity has become a religion without relationship. Relationship arcs together with Yahweh's heart to bring about transformation. I don't attend church just because I want to go to heaven one day or because I want to be presented to the elders or the pastor through my works and effort to prove that I'm faithful and that I'm here. There has to be something more that is happening within our hearts.

Paul says we are going from glory to glory and he says we are ever increasing and expanding. The glory that sits within us as sons has to begin to behold from Yeshua's heart to ours, so we can begin to arc together with Him, go through the gate to begin to stand as an echo chamber of light.

I've been sitting on the subject of being an echo chamber for a while but haven't spoken or written about it because I haven't found the language to truly begin to release and reveal something that's going to bring about a shift, by recognising the nature of Yahweh that is inside of us, which affects the arena that is around us. This nature of Yahweh goes into the atmosphere of the earth, it goes beyond the earth, it goes into the galaxies and stars and planets, and it goes around the celestial arena and into a sphere that Yahweh calls the heavens which is where we operate from. We are not just lesser human beings, sitting within the realm of earth, trying to navigate our heart to Yahweh in the hope that He sees us through the Christian rituals we do which make us feel that we are close to Him or that He is accepting us to some degree. There is so much more that is in store for us, which is why we do what we do.

A shift happens which comes through knowledge and it's this knowledge, through an encounter, which begins to set our mind in motion to realise that there are certain belief systems we have traded into that war against the knowledge of who we are as a son in creation. When we ask those questions and begin to turn ourselves to the truth, the veil is lifted, just like how Paul says that when one turns to the Lord, the veil is lifted. The Bible doesn't say the veil is lifted and then one turns to the Lord. The Bible doesn't say we have to get all this knowledge and understand it and live it and then the veil will be lifted. It talks about a practical turning, to begin to engage so that the veil can be lifted. I've seen this in my life and in the lives of those that I've walked in relationship with and I've seen the struggles where we say we have to get this right, we have to understand it. I've had conversations where people get upset and tense with themselves because they want what someone like Lindi has. I tell them to relax! I tell them they have to come to a place of rest because when we rest and put down our preconceived ideas of where we should be, but we're not, we must realise that we're a lot further than we think we are. It's just that we've been entangled in a system under the sun, in corruption, which is going into decay and is needing a resurrection of an encounter to transform our thinking. Paul talks about this. There is so much truth written in the Scriptures and yet we don't see it because we haven't turned to the Lord. We are still trying to figure things out before we get to grips with what we believe is true for us.

I want to demonstrate how crazy this journey has been for me. I started to engage with the process of learning about the function of my body, going in, beholding, going through gateways and learning how to navigate through myself as a son positioned in Yeshua, and Yeshua in the Father as mentioned in **John 17**. When we are positioned there we begin to navigate who we are as a son. We are wonderfully unique, mystical beings. Scientists haven't figured out how we are designed and created. They've learned certain laws and patterns but there is a depth that they cannot get to because only we, through an encounter, can go through that door to engage with vaults and chambers that are on the inside, that are filled with light waiting to be released and revealed.

We were never designed to live from the outside in. We were designed by the breath of Yahweh to live from the inside out and to begin to behold that place where we live which is who we are within creation. We are a spirit being that has a soul, living in a physical body. We are not a physical body that has a soul with a spirit-man somewhere inside. This is the mindset that so many within the Church Age have because they have entangled themselves in religious belief systems and structures which war against the knowledge of who we are as a son. We get taught that we are a being, a physical body, a human within the earth that has a soul but we never address our spirit-man within the Church Age.

We must understand that when Yahweh engages with us, He engages our spirit. Our soul begins to arc together with our spirit-man allowing the light of our spirit-man to shine through that chamber and emanate into every arena that we sit and govern over.

I get so frustrated when I hear people speak with such disrespect about their souls, even with the knowledge that we have. The soul is such an incredible created being that sits within us waiting for maturity to be revealed to us so we can behold who it is. It's our soul that begins to take what our spirit-man is engaging with and becomes the unique arcing point so it can release that for which our physical bodies have been waiting for. Our physical bodies are not designed just as a physical entity in creation going from bondage to decay, which is the system we've seen under the sun in corruption. We get born, we grow up and at a certain point start deteriorating. When we get to a 'ripe old age' we die and go to heaven. That has been our model. Paul speaks about this subject and there are others in our day that are speaking about the truth of living forever. If we do not speak about this then there is no framework for us to engage, behold and see that this could be possible.

I'm excited to see some of the things the generations that are being born today (especially those that are being born into this mystical tribe and people) are going to see and behold and walk out because they don't have to untangle to the measure and degree that we have had to. There is a purity and clear understanding in who they are and where they operate from that they don't need to be in a religious system and structure in order to find value and to feel fulfilled. They understand that fulfilment comes from their union with Yahweh.

Through this journey, I had to let go of the belief which I had through the law of first mention that I needed to work and make an effort in order to gain the knowledge so I could work everything out. This would take an eternity! There is a grace which rests upon us and that we arc with that gives us the capacity to live from that realm when we begin to trade in honour with those that are walking with in the secrets.

To think, is to go. To see, is to be there. I have been on a ten year journey going through the process of engaging with the protocol of stepping in to behold things and I'm at the stage where I'm able to go to the realms and dimensions of my Father and instantly go to the next universe, the next dimension, the next realm. It's as quick as that because I've learned to navigate through my Father's dimensions, Kingdom and house. I can go there and from that realm I can operate through all the gateways of who I am, and the different beings that I am. There is more than one of me that come through all the processes and gates in who I am and sit within my physical body, waiting for me. This physical body is a chamber of light waiting to be released and revealed. Often, the light that we talk about is a frequency, not a colour, although it can be. Light is a sound and a frequency and eventually our physical body takes on the image of that which it is beholding.

I get so excited about this because I keep saying that we need to see from the inside out. What I've failed to demonstrate is that we cannot afford to behold what is trying to influence us from the outside in. Yeshua operated in this realm. He knew - and we know that He knew - that He was a Son from a different realm, operating from a different dimension and within His physical body, He began to see things being revealed.

Genesis is a book that I've been sitting on, dissecting, going into and allowing it to expand in me as I expand in it. I've been engaging and beholding because the Scriptures in the Bible are not just words on a page, *they are gateways and portals.* This entire book is a vault that we can step into which gives us the understanding and the knowledge, through encounters, which allow us to step into the secret chambers of Yahweh. We can then begin to see things that we cannot see if we aren't positioned through the Scriptures as a physical body here within creation.

The Bible says in **Genesis 1:1-5**, "In the beginning God created the heavens and the earth. The earth was without form, and void; and darkness was on the face of the deep. And the Spirit of God was hovering over the face of the waters. Then God said, 'Let there be light;' and there was light. And God saw the light, that it was good; and God divided the light from the darkness. God called the light Day and the darkness He called Night. So the evening and the morning were the first day."

The night or the darkness that is referred to in this Scripture is *not* evil. Within the church mindset, so many people thought God was separating the good from the bad, the righteous from the unrighteous. No, He was separating something and we have to begin to go through and behold in order to see what was manifesting during this time.

In **Genesis 1:14-19** we read, "Then God said, 'Let there be lights in the firmament of the heavens to divide the day from the night; and let them be for signs and seasons, and for days and years; and let them be for lights in the firmament of the heavens to give light on the earth'; and it was so. Then God made two great lights: the greater light to rule the day, and the lesser light to rule the night. He made the stars also. God set them in the firmament of the heavens to give light on the earth, and to rule over the day and over the night, and to divide the light from the darkness. And God saw that it was good. So the evening and the morning were the fourth day."

In this passage of Scripture, we see that two lights are mentioned. The problem is that this has become entangled within the earth's system and structure. Which light has

Christianity and humanity been sitting under? So many have found themselves under the *lesser* light (the sun) which releases a frequency which we are subjected to because of belief systems that are religious in nature and have entangled us to an earth system that teaches us, through the law of first mention, that we cannot leave earth, that we cannot go to heaven until our physical body dies and only then can we inherit the Kingdom.

The majority, if not all, of humanity has been positioned under a sun that we believe is the light that governs the day. Some say that the moon is the lesser light than governs the night. We've got it all wrong! There is a light here that existed before any *day* was created. God said, "Let there be light," and there was light.

When we go through Yeshua, who is the New and Living Way, and we present ourselves as a physical body there, we can go outside of time and travel to and fro on our timeline. We can go back, we can be present and we can go forward to see what is unfolding because we are outside of the light that is spoken about in **Genesis 1:14**, which is the light of the sun. This is where the framework of time came into existence and we begin to see many things that are written about in **Romans 8** which talks about creation going from bondage to decay and waiting. For what? For us as sons to go through all the gateways and to be established in the realms where we are positioned, back at the beginning, where Yahweh said, "Let there be light." That is where we were. That is where we can have the memory of our created being sitting within the expanse of the light when Yahweh began to frame things.

Light that comes from the sun has interference which creates memory so we can behold and see with our physical sight, but it is still a lesser light. That is the reason Moshe, when he was positioned in the place where Yahweh said, "Let there be light," could begin to write about his death in the third person. In his place of government and being positioned in that arena he could go to and fro to begin to see what was to come. Paul says it is by *faith* that we can begin to trust, believe and have hope for things that are not yet seen. It is by the Being of Faith that the immaturity of humanity can step through and allows us to be lifted up outside of the influence of the sun's light to go beyond and to step into the greatest light that came from the breath of Yahweh when He said in the beginning, "Let there be light." In that position, Yahweh can begin to behold the union that He has with us and we can look into the interference of created light, which creates particles that become solid so we can see and touch them.

When Yeshua was about to be killed by very angry Jews, Scripture says that He walked *through* them. How did He do that? He lived from the light that Yahweh spoke in **Genesis 1**, the light that overshadows any interference that creates particles that become a solid form. Within that light He could begin to step in through Himself and *walk through* solid objects because He had begun to operate from a realm that was superior to the light that the sun emanated.

There is an excitement and joy for the secrets that Yahweh is beginning to release to His creation because we're at a place where we want to behold His image. We don't want to do things by the giftings and mantles through which we build a ministry which enables us to be recognised, known, and accepted in the earth by humanity. We are being transformed into the image and into the likeness of our Father. In **John 20:14-15** we read, "Now when she had said this, she turned around and saw Jesus standing there, and did not know that it was Jesus. Jesus said to her, 'Woman, why are you weeping? Whom are you seeking?' She, supposing Him to be the gardener, said to Him, 'Sir, if You have carried Him away, tell me where You have laid Him, and I will take Him away.'"

Here we read about the time when Yeshua had been resurrected and transfigured. When Mary saw Him, Scripture says that she did not recognise Him. Why? The way we look now is going to change through transformation when we begin to arc with who we are as a spirit-being from before the foundation of the earth.

We were there with Yahweh and Wisdom when they said, "Let there be light." We were beholding what was unfolding in that atmosphere. We are in creation, not just because it was planned by our parents, but because we were beholding what was happening under the sun and said at the exact right time we want to come into creation. Yahweh wrote our testimony scroll for us before the foundation of the earth and we agreed to this scroll and said we have to be part of this process, we have to be here right now. We are here to transform the world and creation to a measure which I don't believe has been revealed as yet.

In **Genesis 1:2** we read, "The earth was without form, and void; and darkness was on the face of the deep. And the Spirit of God was hovering over the face of the waters." We know now what the 'darkness' is. Back in 2019 we saw the Face of the Deep begin to stir when sons were engaging and now we're walking out the fruit of what took place within that time.

The word 'hover' means to vibrate. *Ruach haKodesh*, the Spirit of Yahweh, was hovering over the waters creating a frequency through the vibration and He began to arc with the surface of the deep. All the particles and everything inside the surface of the deep started to resound with the same frequency that *Ruach haKodesh* was emitting and came into union with the glorious sound and from that place Yahweh said, "Let there be light" and began to frame and speak the most extravagant light that has ever been displayed. He then separated light from darkness and began to allow the darkness to be hidden for a time. Sons are now engaging with it and the light that is within is beginning to shine in the secrets and mysteries we are revealing to humanity, which have not yet been revealed in creation.

In Scripture, Paul wrote about things he saw in the future. We can have relationship and engage, speak and arc together with those who are in the Kingdom Realms because they're more alive than we think they are! I was engaging with Paul, walking some personal things out in my testimony scroll, when he put his arm around me and said, "Ricky, do you know that the majority of the Scriptures that I wrote should have already been fulfilled, but the religious spirit has kept people thinking it's still coming?" He dropped that statement within me and a good example of this is when I look at the Scripture in **Romans 8**. The Bible says that all creation is waiting for the revealing of sons, for creation was subjected to frustration, not by its own choice, but by the will of the one who subjected it, in the hope that creation will be taken from bondage to decay to be taken into the glorious liberty of the children of Yahweh.

Are we going to read that portion of Scripture for another thousand years, teaching generations that are still coming into creation that this must still come to pass because we are not choosing to engage with this truth? We are trying to frame and teach things that are completely contradicting what Yahweh framed about them before the foundation of the earth. We're going to teach them that a rapture is going to take place to take them out of this world. Are we going to teach them that there is really no future and we just have to trust, through our works and effort, that we're ok before the cross so when we die or the rapture comes, we can be with Him? Are we going to model that for the next generation? Or are we going to teach them that their testimony scroll is a book that is being written.

Paul was navigating through some things and was dealing with issues within his community   and seeing within the light that Yahweh spoke when He said, "Let there be light." In **2 Corinthians 3:1-3** he wrote, "Do we begin again to commend ourselves? Or do we need, as some others, epistles of commendation to you or letters of commendation from you? You are our epistle written in our hearts, known, and read by all men; clearly you are an epistle of Christ, ministered by us, written not with ink but by the Spirit of the living God, not on tablets of stone but on tablets of flesh, that is, of the heart."

This is the very Spirit who hovered and vibrated over the surface of the deep, the Spirit of Yahweh, that Paul is saying is beginning to stir up things within us because of what is written upon our hearts. He carries on in **verse 4-6** and says, "And we have such trust through Christ toward God. Not that we are sufficient of ourselves to think of anything as being from ourselves, but our sufficiency is from God, who also made us sufficient as ministers of the new covenant, not the letter but of the Spirit; for the letter kills, but the Spirit gives life."

I have seen so many people who are scared of going through these processes to encounter things. There should be no fear of encounters. If we are engaging with a fear that is allowing us to believe it's not our portion because we're too scared to be deceived, or because we've seen others being deceived, I'm going to set you free through an encounter that I had, so that you no longer question if your encounters, and what you're engaging with, are from Yahweh.

The letter Paul was referring to in **2 Corinthians 3** is that we should never read this portion of Scripture through works and effort, we should never read this connected to the religious spirit because if we do that we will not have the Spirit of life attached to it and it will allow us to step into Christian rituals.

In **2 Corinthians 3:7-13** Paul writes, "But if the ministry of death, written and engraved on stones, was glorious, so that the children of Israel could not look steadily at the face of Moses because of the glory of his countenance, which glory was passing away, how will the ministry of the Spirit not be more glorious? For if the ministry of condemnation had glory, the ministry of righteousness exceeds much more in glory. For even what was made glorious had no glory in this respect, because of the glory that excels. For if what is passing away was glorious, what remains is much more glorious. Therefore, since we have such hope, we use great boldness of speech— unlike Moshe, who put a veil over his face so that the children of Israel could not look steadily at the end of what was passing away."

The ministry of condemnation speaks about the law which people needed to obey and required them to do works. Many of us have read this Scripture and asked ourselves why Moshe threw a cloth over himself. It wasn't a cloth! The people couldn't come near him because they were so afraid of the countenance of Yahweh that was on Moshe because he came back looking like Yahweh! Moshe had to step out of that realm and through a 'veil' in order to present himself to his people in his physical body, and the glory began to fade. Paul says we will not be like Moshe because there is no more law, so we don't have to tell people to be careful of us if we become like Yahweh in case they look at us and die. We should now have the perfect union, through the relationship with Yeshua, the New and Living Way, to present ourselves as living sons to Yahweh, to become like Him. Paul is saying we will not be like Moshe who had to veil himself to present himself to the people. I believe that in the state the Israelites were in that they would have all died.

2 Corinthians 3:14-18 says, "But their minds were blinded. For until this day, the same veil remains unlifted in the reading of the Old Testament because the veil is taken away in Christ. But even to this day, when Moses is read, a veil lies on their heart. Nevertheless, when one turns to the Lord, the veil is taken away. Now the Lord is the Spirit; and where the Spirit of the Lord is, there is liberty. But we all, with unveiled face, beholding as in a mirror the glory of the Lord, are being transformed into the same image from glory to glory, just as by the Spirit of the Lord."

I know people who say they love Jesus but are living their life through works and effort as they step into this religious place and they look unhappy. Paul says that the Spirit we engage with brings life. Don't read the letters bound in law because it kills.

I speak so passionately about the sinners prayer or the prayer of salvation because it is man-made and gives Christians a hope *for* the future because they are too scared to go through an encounter and live *from* the future.

The Lord is Spirit and what Paul is saying here is that through ascension and through our position and union that we have when we operate from that place of government, Yahweh begins to speak to us spirit to spirit because that is how it was always designed to be before the foundation of the earth. We were there when Yahweh said, "Let there be light."

My mountain is open to all your mountains to engage within this process so I invite you to explore this, dissect it, engage with it as I'm only speaking about things I have engaged with. This will transform your life when you realise that you are positioned above the sun, operating from a different source of light, which is the most incredible light that was framed from the breath of Yahweh that came from the Spirit of Yahweh hovering over the surface of the deep. You are positioned within that light when you walk within creation. You govern over the record of the light that the sun creates because you have a law that supersedes that law as it is positioned within the union and relationship with Yahweh. Remember that when you speak, frame and create.

Chapter 2

Sharing Breath

Rick and I have been doing these conferences because we have a heart to get people to understand, from our point of view, what it looks like to engage and to step into the fulness of these realms. I'm acutely aware that this decade of rest, this era that we walked into on 22 December 2021 when the seraphim came in, is the decade where we learn to walk into this final thirteenth age. You and I agreed to be here and we're learning how to be these breathing, living beings that take us right back to **Genesis 1** when Yahweh spoke to *Ish* and *Isha* and told them He wanted them to be fruitful, to multiply and replenish. We are able to be fruitful and multiply but we're not so good at replenishing. This is our decade to learn how to replenish, how to put back and to re-instate.

In **Chapter 2** of Genesis, the Bible says Yahweh rested on the seventh day. This was not because He was exhausted but because He had found a man to do the job. Nowhere between Genesis and Revelation does Yahweh say that He'll take that mandate away from us. In the Church age and especially amongst Charismatic people within the Church age, we've adopted the narrative that we're waiting for someone to come in on a white horse and save the day and to help us to fix everything. We're always looking at the sky and waiting for Him to come and make everything right. He never said He would do that. He said all power has been given to Me, and now YOU go.

The Bible tells us in **John 14:12** that because He is in us, we now have the power to do the things He did and that we will do greater works. We love that idea but even in "the greater works" we are still waiting for someone to come and save the day and do the greater works through us. In other words, we still say we're just the lowly vessel and that it's not about us it's about Him as He works through us. We must grow up and mature and what Rick and I are doing through this series addresses maturity. I always say maturity is our *Vav* which hooks us into creation so that creation can turn and look at us and say, "I have been waiting, not willingly, but in subjection to, futiliy." Subjected to what? Subjected to waiting for SONS to manifest who are also waiting for their bodies to manifest so that we can get on with replenishing. **Romans 8:19-20**, creation was subjected, not willingly, but it was subjected to wait for the glorious revelation of the sons who were made a little lower than Elohim.

As much as I love the charismatic roots that I come from, which I've been in for forty-one years, there's been a debilitating thing that has happened within this movement in the last fifteen to twenty years where we've lost the power and the ability to do what we had been doing because we're still waiting for God's man of power for the hour. I guarantee you that if I said that tomorrow at 3 a.m. a powerful prophet was coming online who can tell you the secrets of your heart and can tell you what's coming in the future, I would have six hundred people on that forum at 3 a.m. to hear what he has to say. It's still engrained in our DNA that we're waiting for God's man of power for the hour.

I don't despise prophecy. I travelled as a prophet and I love prophetic words, but honestly, I don't live for them and I don't wait for them any longer. I would go to meetings in my capacity as a prophet and would see people wearing bright colours hoping that I would pick them out of the crowd and then there were the people who were terrified I'd see something and were hiding behind the sound desk. Year after year it was the same thing. I knew there was a new way that we could operate in, seeing our scrolls from our future. I love to give prophecies and could give prophetic words any time of the day because that is the gift that is in me, but it's exhausting to have people wait to hear about their future from a prophet or waiting to be healed because an evangelist who heals is coming to town. We've got to get to a place of maturity where we can begin to access things for ourselves which is why Rick and I do this, and why Ian and Dr O do this. We're trying to bring ourselves and our people to a place of maturity so that we can walk through walls, translocate, raise the dead, etc.

Some within our tribe have been talking about sharing breath and as I have begun to engage with this, I have received understanding as they have given me the theology behind what I've been doing. In **John 20:21-22** Scripture says, "So Jesus said to them again, "Peace to you! As the Father has sent Me, I also send you." And when He had said this, He breathed on them, and said to them, "Receive the Holy Spirit."

It's interesting how the breath that He breathed is what created the ability for them to receive the *Ruach haKodesh*. I looked up the words 'breathed on them' in Greek which is to blow or breathe upon or to share breath. Yeshua breathed on them, shared breath with them and *Ruach haKodesh* came upon them.

In **Genesis 2:7** we read, "And the Lord God formed man of the dust of the ground, and breathed into his nostrils the

25

breath of life; and man became a living being." In Hebrew 'breathed into his nostrils' is *napah* which means: to breathe; to blow or to blow upon; to cause to breathe out; like a furnace that is blown upon so that it lights up. He breathed upon him and he became a living being. We know that Adam did this when he named the animals. The Jews teach that they 'blow the breath' to give life when they name things or people. When we say the letter *Alef*, it's more of a breathy sound than a guttural sound. When we say the *Yud Hey Vav Hey*, we breathe in and out. His name is breath because breath is life. Breathing is very important and I believe we haven't fully engaged with it within our Christian walk.

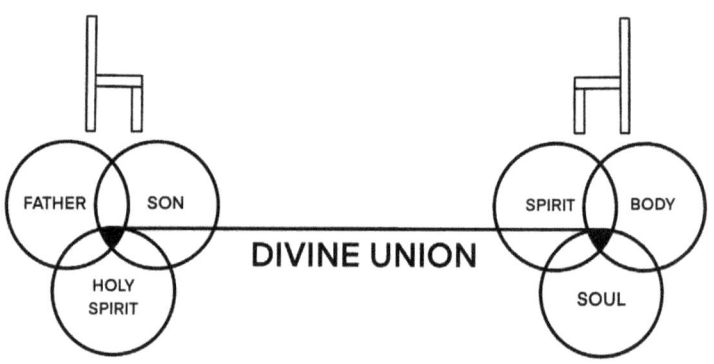

If I draw intersecting circles to represent the Father, the Son, and the Holy Spirit, and another set of intersecting circles representing myself made up of spirit, soul, and body, I know that on top of each set of circles sits a throne with Yahweh on His throne and myself on my throne. A divine union happens in the middle of the concentric circles. We are able to break an ungodly soul-tie between our spirit, soul and body in order for us to come into divine union. **Hebrews 4:12**, Jesus said that I am in You and You are in Me, together with Holy Spirit, and they are in Us. There is an 'in Us' that happens within these circles – the Father in union with our spirit, the Son in union with our soul and Holy Spirit in union with our body and this makes our temple, or body, holy. Divine union takes place between the Father, the Son and the Holy Spirit and our three-part body. The 'body' is the last frontier because we've held the body in derision through not being taught that our body is holy. The Jews call our bodies the palace of divine holiness and the new covenant calls it the temple of the Holy Spirit. The Bible says we must put on Christ and we do this as we breathe and say Y-H-V-H to the Father. He takes that breath and puts it back into us so through that synergy of shared breath where we can say that we have put on Christ. Christ in us the hope of glory. **Colossians 1:27**. We become one through divine union.

Our breath and speech form and create things from one realm into another realm, calling those things which be not as though they are. **Romans 4:17b**. I once used the phrase "in the name of Jesus" like a magic wand when I wanted to do something or pray for someone. This is why we've been so powerless! We're still waiting for the magic wand of "in the name of Jesus" to work! A huge number of Christians have walked away from Jesus and the Church in disillusionment because hope deferred makes the heart sick. We've prayed for healing and have not seen it; we've prayed for money and have not seen it; we've tithed but things haven't changed. We've done all these things, received prophecies that haven't been fulfilled, we've heard things from God which have never happened and so we leave because we just don't think it works. A pastor friend of mine is now an atheist. I was shattered at the terrible things he posted online about God and in his case, hope deferred made his heart so sick that he walked away. He had built his ministry on his personality and what he thought he knew about the Word, but there was no experiential gospel and no encounter. Everything Ricky and I do is because of encounters we have had.

Before I left South Africa ten years ago, I knew I was going to hand this ministry over to Ricky. In fact we were training him up from way before because he was our Timothy. When I left the country I was worried about how he was going to cope because he was only in his mid-twenties, but I knew Yahweh had spoken to us. A few years later Ricky and I were in New Zealand at a conference with Ian Clayton where he told the folk that when he had taken over the Church he wasn't a Christian but had subsequently had an encounter and then became a Son. Ricky had turned from a Christian into a Christ-follower. He had become a man who was now walking from a place of encounter. I believe that's the difference between becoming a Christian by repeating the sinner's prayer and being one who is Born From Above through an encounter with Christ.

I often stress to parents not to lead their small children to Jesus through the prayer of salvation. They MUST have a divine encounter. It's this encounter that keeps us in Him when things are tough. The prayer of salvation started getting used in the first few decades of the nineteen-hundreds by Billy Sunday and then Billy Graham started using it for his crusades when thousands of people were getting saved by saying that prayer. Later it became a popular means for churches to use it in their meetings or even on TV broadcasts. This prayer does not necessarily ground people in Yahweh, so when difficult times come or they're being really sinful, they say it again which creates a cycle of backsliding and coming back thus making Christians feel like hopeless losers because they haven't learned how to walk within encounter. When we have an encounter with Jesus Christ of Nazareth, and His blood, nothing takes us away from Him.

Ever. No matter if someone hurts us, or if someone we love dearly does something bad, we would still love him and walk with him because of an encounter.

Sharing breath is about encounter. When Adam gave the animals their names, he didn't look at each animal and decide to name them according to what they looked like. He got a name and breathed it out over the creature who then received its characteristics according to the name it was given. It was its name that gave it its character. The same applies to us when we are in the womb. Our parents don't know our characteristics but the name we receive from them is what creates our characteristics. This is why it's good to know our name both here on earth and the one in heaven.

We speak those things that be not as though they are by breathing and speaking them into life. If we're standing as sons, we can even *think* it into life. Through breath we create a womb for what we want to see happen in creation. Our breath creates a birthing process in the womb of who we are. As we begin to breathe into Him and share breath with Him in divine union we can turn and breathe onto the face of the earth because of the birthing process of the breath which sits within us – not just of what's already in existence, but also of what is to come. This is called terraforming.

One of the ways to terraform is through worshipping Yahweh in Spirit and truth. Many of the songs we sing in the Church Age are about ourselves and our circumstances and not about Him or to Him so we're literally worshipping ourselves. We've disconnected our intellect because of the songs we sing, which keep us so earthbound. When we sing in tongues and sing Y-H-V-H in a corporate setting, an arcing takes place between us which goes up into the realms of the Kingdom, where He inhabits the praises of His people, and comes back down again. Through our breath, we're singing in the Spirit and terraforming and creating. Because Yahweh inhabits our praises, everything that He is and has, starts to be released onto the face of the earth.

We know that in many of the great revivals that have happened around the world, things have happened. In the natural there's often a download into creation of technology and the Christians all run towards the revival while the world sees the technology and create something. They became millionaires because the rain falls on the righteous and the unrighteous. We then look at them and wonder why they're prospering and we aren't. The Charismatic Church Age has taught us to run to revivals instead of asking the Father what we can terraform.

As we share breath with Him we land something on the face of the earth because we are terraforming with our breath. When we pray, when we speak in tongues, when we do the Y-H-V-H, when we hum – the letter *Mem* is a humming sound – we are creating something because we're using breath. The Word says to meditate day and night and meditating is the "mmmm" sound which releases the *Mem* into the upper and lower waters.

We use sonship to see what is coming, catch it and form it onto the face of the earth. We, as humanity, are currently in our fourth estate and Yahweh wants to bring us back to a new heaven and a new earth which is going to be the ninth day of creation and can only come through mature sons. We're living in the eighth day and about to step into the ninth day which is clearly written about in **Romans 8**. This act of terraforming is happening because in our prayer, meditations, singing, and worship, the breath of our mouth is released and He can bring the change on the face of the earth through us.

We cannot terraform what is coming if we cannot see it. We have to see it in our hearts and spirits and begin to form it in our imagination. **Imagination is disciplined formation.** In other words, when we have an undisciplined imagination and it's all over the place and we've seen all sorts of things that don't come to pass we get into a place of being disappointed because hope deferred makes our heart sick. Our imagination needs to be linked into divine union, arcing with Yeshua, so that we can arc with our imagination which in turn becomes disciplined formation - the forming of something.

My family and I have seen a property that we're trusting for and because I find myself in this place of union with Yahweh I'm constantly in a place of disciplined imagination, framing through breath and imagination, because my imagination is in a godly place. I imagine what the house is going to look like, what we're going to use it for and why we need it. Every time I go past the property, I breathe over it and I say to it, "I'm here. I know you need us to come in and take over." It's not an impossibility but at the moment it's not available and I believe we will get it because of disciplined formation and speaking life over it, calling it into our domain and into what Yahweh wants to do with us and through us by creating an arc. Many of us have been told to stop using our imagination and even in church we've been told that it's demonic and if something isn't in the Bible, we can't access it. We need to untangle ourselves from that by going into our DNA and pulling out the lies surrounding our imagination and bring it back to a godly place, covered in the blood of the Lamb.

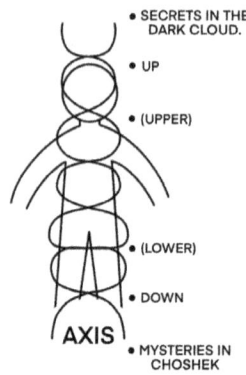

- SECRETS IN THE DARK CLOUD.
- UP
- (UPPER)
- (LOWER)
- DOWN

AXIS
- MYSTERIES IN CHOSHEK

Learning how to breathe is key in formation. We know we have the up and down axis. The lower is where we have the mysteries and the upper is where we find the secrets of Yahweh. The mysteries are in the *choshek* and the secrets are in the dark cloud of the Lord. The up and down process is us engaging in meditation by speaking in tongues and engaging with the living letters and if we had to see this in picture form we would see a spiralling taking place between the upper and lower waters, travelling up and down in constant motion between the secrets and the mysteries, in the up and the down, as we speak in tongues and engage with Yahweh in the realms of the Kingdom and share breath with the Y-H-V-H in meditation with *Ruach*. Yeshua starts to do something – there's an ascension, whether we feel it or not – our spirit and soul start to arc and spiral as they reach into the choshek and into the dark cloud of the Lord, arcing through us into creation.

The mysteries are on the face of the earth because they are in printed form in the Bible while the secrets are there for us to find. It is the glory of our Father to conceal the secrets and the honour of the kings to seek them out. I believe that in this decade we will begin to access the secrets of Yahweh. Meditation, speaking in tongues and engaging with the living letters are keys. We also know about two of the hidden letters, the *Ghah*, hidden in the *Ayin* and the *Shin Gadol*, hidden in the *Shin*. These are the two ascension letters that Yahweh has released in recent years so we can learn how to live an ascended life.

How do we share breath with the Y-H-V-H? It's the breathing in and out of His name. On the in breath we speak Y-H and on the out breath, we speak V-H. I actually stepped into His name and when I did that, He didn't move, He just stood there. Scripture says in Him I live and move and have my being. I found myself IN HIM in divine union. As I realised that I involuntarily breathed in and thought to myself, "I think I've just swallowed Him!" God leaned over me and asked, "What do you want, son?" and I remember thinking that He thought I was Yeshua. That is exactly what it's supposed to look like! We must be so entrenched in Yeshua that when Yahweh looks at us, He sees a whole lot of Yeshua's running around. I'm with Him, I'm in Him, I'm encased in Him, I'm cloaked in Him.

It is Yeshua haMashiach who creates our boundaries which means we cannot do what we want. As we operate within those boundaries and begin to speak in tongues, He creates the boundaries of what will be created in the ninth day, which is the new heaven and the new earth. Those boundaries are within ourselves so if we are in Him we will never step outside of those boundaries because as long as our imagination is brought into a disciplined formative place we can do anything. Our imagination is a divine ancient gateway that Yahweh restored a number of years ago and has allowed us to walk through and to create.

My husband owned a copy of a book that John G. Lake wrote

and as he engaged with what was written there he made some notes which said, "If I want to live the Christ-life, I must become a Christ-man." John G. Lake knew that to be able to create in the ninth day, within the boundaries set for us, we HAVE to put on the Christ-man in order to live the Christ-life so that Yeshua can present us to the Father and when we look at Yahweh we can become a god-man. The Magi, were called god-men, as was Enoch called a god-man because all of his six bodies had arced together. The ancient texts report that people were scared of Enoch when he came down through portals because he had become a god-man. They asked him to stop talking to them because his face terrified them. Enoch and Moses had become god-men. This is our bread and our portion which is why Ricky and I do what we do. This is working because Yahweh is urging us and saying we are a little lower than Him.

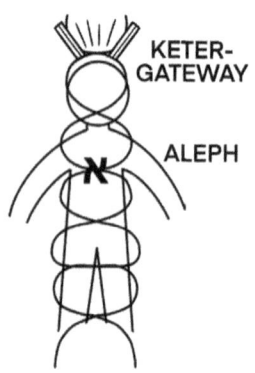

When we share breath with each living letter we see that each one has a paleo form. The *Alef* for example has a picture of an ox which means the head, the leader or strength. Each letter also has a colour, a shape, a sound, a frequency and a number. As each letter has a sound or a frequency I would like to suggest that when we hear the planets singing it is because Yahweh created the planets through the living letters (because they are formative) and it is them that hold the universe together bringing the Father, the breath, Yeshua and Holy Spirit together and what we hear is their frequency!

At one meeting we were going into the Courts of Heaven and a young boy who I know said he did this differently to us. He was eight years old. He went through the letter *Qof* and when he got through the seventh layer of heaven he saw his family's scroll which he took to a classroom. He told me he saw frequencies and colours and was then introduced to each of the Seven Spirits of Yahweh.

When we share breath with the living letters our spirit engages with each one off the letters. If we choose to engage with the letter *Alef*, we look at it and breath the name *Alef*. The letter then breathes our breath. *Alef* sits within the human body in the general throat area where the thyroid is. When we string the letters together in our body we see that they run along these lines holding our body together with the tree of life on our inside. As I share breath with *Alef* it releases its meaning which is strength, ox, leader. When we breathe Y-H-V-H by bringing it through our gateway at the top of our head and into our body, sharing breath and letting it out again, our body gets healed. This is how we bring healing to our body and how we can begin to terraform our own bodies.

With our spirit, we engage each letter by praying in the Spirit. Speaking in tongues is so important because it edifies us but there's a difference between speaking in tongues and praying in the Spirit. Our spirit, which sits inside us, knows everything which is under and above the sun, whether we remember it or not. As we unfold the realm of Yahweh around us we then turn and unfold the realm that is above us. We don't have to sit under the sun all the time. Some of the mysteries might sit under the sun which do not make them bad or evil but actually give us a platform to read into the secrets of Yahweh.

When I share breath with the living letters, I sometimes say the following:
Y-H *Alef* V-H, Y-H *Beyt* V-H, Y-H *Gimel* V-H, Y-H *Dalet* V-H, Y-H *Hey* V-H. Sometimes I change the pattern and beat and in so doing I am sharing breath with them and bringing their frequency and vibration into myself. It will get to a stage when I'll be able to walk through walls. I've done it once before! As I engage my body starts to flow into and out of their realm and the waters of my body starts to vibrate because all the letters are strung together on the inside. There are ten spiritual points on the inside of us plus we have the twenty-two letters which brings the total to thirty-two which the Jews call the thirty-two pathways of wisdom. They're waiting for us to activate them through the disciplined formation of our imagination by opening each door, sharing breath with them so that a vibration and frequency can be released in us and terraforming begins to happen and we can start to speak life and call those things that be not as though they are. That's when we can start creating.

When we're engaging with going up and down and praying in the spirit, the mysteries in the *choshek* in the lower waters and the secrets in the dark cloud of the Lord start unfolding into the face of the earth but not so that we can keep them for ourselves. As we engage on the face of the earth, wherever we are, something shifts and our attention is directed to the dark cloud of the Lord and into the secrets of Yahweh. As this begins to sit in us, the action of formation happens because our sonship begins to create and to form around us here on the face of the earth and then the earth begins to turn towards us. When we step outside our door, the earth and the people need to notice us coming. Trees need to see us coming as sons. They are waiting for our frequency as sons to manifest.

When we bought our house, everything was broken. My builder asked me recently why I get upset when my plants get broken and I told him that there were no plants when I bought the house and I planted all the greenery that is there now. As my garden took shape, my neighbour's plants grew under the fence and into my yard because they all wanted to grow in my yard. My swimming pool holds 125 000 litres of water and whenever I'm listening to a teaching or engaging it starts to behave strangely – the whole body of water starts to move to and fro and splashes over the brickwork. We don't live in an earthquake zone. The only way I can stop it is to switch on the pool pump so the water circulates instead of splashing over the sides. The waters are singing because I'm so very aware of the inner waters, the *Mem* that sits in my belly. As I begin to meditate and engage the pool water responds. Likewise, the trees and insects also respond. That is how it should be because of terraformation. If we grow vegetables we can breathe over them and they must respond.

Our body has breath and shares breath with our spirit which also has breath. Our spirit is a living entity and part of who we are as divine beings. When we pray in the Spirit – not in tongues – we start sharing breath with our spirit and as we speak and breathe out our spirit breathes in and starts speaking back into our body. Back in the day when Ricky and I would preach in the Church Age we would say that we've suddenly got a download from heaven because we didn't know where our words came from. My husband used to do that often and would have to listen to a recording of his message because he said things that he had never heard before. That is sharing breath. That is when our spirit turns to Holy Spirit while speaking in tongues and Holy Spirit says, "Yes! I have an avenue through which to speak," and He speaks in us and through us, downloading the upper waters into us and it comes through our mouth.

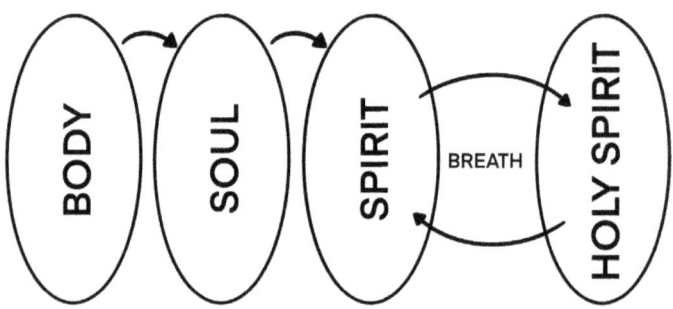

Synergy takes place; I speak through my mouth to my spirit, my spirit speaks to Holy Spirit, Holy Spirit speaks and shares breath with my spirit and there is a download from heaven. When I share breath with my spirit it breathes in and starts to speak with Holy Spirit – *Ruach haKodesh* – who begins to help me in my weaknesses. That word is actually translated incorrectly because it should be read as infirmities. This not only means in our sicknesses but also where we have lack. It is also in that place where Holy Spirit makes groanings with sounds that cannot be uttered and He begins to intercede on our behalf and prays the perfect will of God over our life. When people ask what the perfect will of God is for their lives, they need to share breath with Holy Spirit because He will pray it for them and they will walk out their destiny scroll.

I love the fact that I share breath because **Proverbs 18:21** says that there is life and death in the power of the tongue. Our words carry breath and are terraforming both good and evil and those that love it will eat the fruit of it. We must watch what we say which is why I keep talking about walking through walls because I know how to share breath. When we come into divine union with the *Ruach haKodesh* then our spirit breathes the mysteries of Yahweh into existence. The mysteries come out of our mouth.

As we sit, as a spirit being, at the door of the Word (just because we love the mysteries does not mean we do not engage with the Word) and the living letters and the paleo forms, we then begin to engage within that letter, waiting in expectation to share breath with that letter whilst praying in the Spirit and waiting for that letter to speak or breathe back which takes us to a place where we are fully engaging. Once I'm fully engaged with that letter I can practice releasing formation which starts to change the earth.

As an example, let us take these three living letters in their paleo form: *Hey* who has a gematria of 5, *Aleph* is 1 and *Dalet* is 4. As we meditate on these letters it's good to have our feet on the ground because I like to be grounded in creation because it is through the *malkuth* that we stand and our maturity is our *Vav* into creation. We will breathe in for five counts, holding the breath on *Hey* and looking at all the elements of that letter which means to behold, to reveal, to breathe. Next, we hold *Aleph* within us and look at the ox, the leader, strength, and then we breathe out for the count of four, engaging with the *Dalet* which is a door.

To recap:
Breathe in for five counts meditating on *Hey*. Hold for one count and concentrate on *Aleph*. Breathe out for four counts and think on *Dalet*. Repeat twice more.
When I do this meditation I am saying the following: Behold

the ox, the leader, as I step through the door of His Kingdom. The same can be done with the Y-H-V-H. The living letters realize someone is sharing breath with them, that a son wants to engage with them. What is the purpose of sharing breath with the living letters? Through meditation, speaking in tongues, and through the living letters we bring all of creation through the doorway of the imagination with a disciplined formation to terraform the earth so that we get this place ready to turn it into its ninth day – a new heaven and a new earth. This is the decade for us to learn how to do this. Remember that every time we speak, we share breath, both good and bad. We must become aware of what we speak.

Chapter 3
Living Beyond The Veil

I've been walking some things through in my own life regarding living beyond the veil but there is actually no veil because in **2 Corinthians 3:14** we read, "But their minds were blinded. For until this day, the same veil remains unlifted in the reading of the Old Testament, because the veil is taken away in Christ." As we exist within creation and understand our roles and functions of government within the Kingdom Realms an arcing takes place as we speak in part and in parables. This is to get sons to understand who they are so they can begin to arc with their minds to know that we should be living from a different realm. We also have to understand that this truth we're walking out is forever increasing. I believe that through encounters truth is multi-dimensional. The truth that I am engaging with today is becoming reality because my maturity is arcing with me in the measure that I am guarding what Yahweh has begun to reveal to me. I'm stepping into and beholding truth which is ever increasing. I'm not saying that the truth I was beholding a year ago is not true, it is true, but there is a greater truth, a truer truth that we are beholding within this journey of maturity.

The veil was torn when Yeshua transitioned through death. We know that Scripture says He died, but we also know, through our encounters and union with Him, that He passed through death and restored death so that it does not have the power it had prior to the cross. We, as sons, can engage with this life that is within Christ. There is no more veil as we understand it and **Hebrews 10:19** says something very significant regarding the veil that is now torn. In the moment that the physical veil hanging in the temple was torn, Yeshua positioned Himself as the New and Living Way that Paul talks about in the book of Hebrews. It is His flesh, His body, which is the New and Living Way. Just as we are, through an encounter, we are seated in Him and with Him which gives us access into the Dimensions and the Realms of the Kingdom.

I find it so hard not to share my encounters and experiences with others but timing is so important. If we speak about things prematurely they don't carry the record of transformation for humanity as they should. When we understand that we are in union with Yeshua and we are stepping into a place that we can now live from, we can come as we are. So many people have beliefs that are entangled and entrenched in a religious system and think they have to deal with their junk before they can behold the Kingdom. If that were the case then no one would ever see God! If we see God in our fallen corrupted state, then yes, we will die. That happened prior to Yeshua transitioning through death and restoring the frequency to life that we are now positioned in that gives us complete access into the Kingdom Realms, so that we can begin to behold the countenance of Yahweh to become like Him. Paul addresses this issue and says that we are gods. This is as a result of the process we have gone through to hold our union and position in Yeshua so we can behold the Kingdom.

The year 2019 was such an incredible year for me. I was travelling quite a bit with various folk that I walk in union with and I remember Ian speaking about the importance of our body while sharing some of the secrets he had received regarding this subject. One particular thing that

Ian mentioned made me take note and my wife and I looked at each other and agreed to trade a substantial amount into the phrase that he had spoken. When we did the trade I felt something happen to me and I was able to behold some truths regarding humanity who, in the process of maturity, can step through Yeshua, who has become the portal and the New and Living Way, and move within the Kingdom and frequency and nature of Yeshua. We can go into all dimensions within our Father's house.

I had to undo and untangle some mindsets I had when reading the Old Testament because I didn't know how to read those Scriptures through my position in Yeshua. I used to ask Yahweh why things happened to people when they even touched the Ark of the Covenant. They dropped dead! The Church at large has entangled itself in the religious belief system and structure that we need to fear God because we have viewed Him from a wrong position, entrenched in the system of the earth, not understanding our function in Yeshua which is understood through an encounter and which gives us the access to explore the fullness of the Kingdom without limitations. The Church has limited the fullness of the Kingdom through a religious man-made prayer, the prayer of salvation or the sinner's prayer, which gives Christians the security *for* a future instead of living *from* the future, as a son, into creation. The religious spirit is not a lesser part of Yahweh's Kingdom – it's a demon! This is why we should not tolerate the religious spirit, or the systems and structures that war against the knowledge of who we are.

When I saw the corrupted seed line within people in the Old Testament, I realized they could not go near the presence, and yet, through Yeshua, Yahweh has given us access into the fullness of the Kingdom and even though there are still corrupted things within our physical body Yahweh says we can come BOLDLY to the Throne of Grace. How is that possible? Yahweh told me why. When we come into His presence, we can bring the fullness of the Kingdom to begin to eliminate corruption on the face of the earth. This would not be possible if we cannot dwell with Him.

What is our function? Before the foundation of the earth, in the beginning, we were with Yahweh and with Wisdom when He said, "Let there be light." We agreed to our function and our scroll because we engaged with the process and were present at that time. When we speak about these things our scroll resonates and vibrates within us because it remembers the frequency of that light and where we are from. Scripture says we are *in* this world but we are not *of* it! A religious thought process has created a veil between us and Yahweh and that veil was the very thing that Paul was addressing when he said the only way the veil is taken away is by turning and beholding Yahweh. We are seated in creation right now even though there is corruption and the world is in a fallen state, but we carry the record of transformation. Yahweh told me that He allowed me to step in through His Son so that I could behold the fullness of His house, and He told me that all the dimensions are mine so I can become like Him even though I might think I am still in a corrupted state within my body, which is going through a process of being transformed and transfigured. He still grants us, through His Son, access to all His dimensions because when we behold it, there's a possibility that creation can do an end with corruption. We are the transition point and the arcing point to allow the corrupted fallen state of the earth to bow in surrender to us because we are in Him.

My journey began when I started reading **Romans 8** and

understanding that we live from a different realm because the veil has been taken away. Yeshua is now the portal and transition point that we step through so we can have full access to the Kingdom. Yahweh does not see our corruption and sin because we are in Christ, positioned in Yeshua. When we are in Him we are positioned as a being of purity, in righteousness, having access to the dimensions and layers that are forever unfolding within our Father's house. We have full access to keys to all the doors, vaults and chambers. Every time we behold and engage it is possible for us to be in a different realm so that our spirit-man can engage in our Father's Kingdom while our physical body is the *Vav* which anchors us into the earth. By understanding that our function is within our union with Yahweh and Yeshua, arcing with *Vav* into creation, we can release what Yahweh has for us in our scroll. It resonates because it's the empowerment of the life that He spoke through His breath that created the scroll while we were there in a co-labouring relationship and we wrote it together to see the fulfilment of what is unfolding.

During the build-up to 22 December 2021 I had an encounter. I was positioned within the place of government where I operate from and I saw creation put a demand upon the Realms of Yahweh's Kingdom for sons to be revealed because creation has been waiting and longing for this day. Creation is not waiting for more churches to be planted. Creation is not waiting for more ministries to be started so that a voice can be heard by others who are engaging with social media. Creation is waiting for the unveiling and revealing of sons so that it can behold us as we behold it, as we arc with the echo chamber of light that Yahweh spoke in **Genesis 1** when He said, "Let there be light." We were there and that light is superior to any other light and it sits in the core of who we are, in the centre of our being.

I was at a conference and through our unity and the government that was in the room we were able to engage with and behold the sun as a living Being. I only go when Yahweh says I can go, not just so that I can have a good spiritual encounter to share with others. Prior to that encounter I was still trying to figure out what was a Being and what wasn't whereas today, everything is a Being until proven otherwise. During the conference, when we engaged with the sun, some folk went into the Being and others (like myself) remained halfway up the mountain. I felt like Joshua because I didn't think I'd come out of that experience alive. A while later, because of a process of maturity, I had another opportunity to engage with the sun as a Being. This time I went through a gate to behold what the sun is made of. I realised that the sun is a created Being in creation waiting for the revealing of sons. When I went through that gate I stepped into the position of government that I carry and began to look at the sun from my perspective. This was the first time I had an encounter where I saw that I was truly living above the sun.

As I was governing in my position as a king and engaging with some legislating the sun began to turn and engage with me and with the light I was positioned in, the very same one when Yahweh said at the beginning, "Let there be light." I found myself in a chamber with the others who were with me in this encounter and we were sitting around a table releasing a frequency. As we hovered together as a tribe and a people, the sun, which had been bringing chaos, turned to look at us and the greater light and started to change its frequency towards all of creation.

I was part of one church for approximately twenty years, serving in various capacities, and during that time witnessed some incredible signs, wonders and miracles. I saw gold dust fall and heard angels singing and engaging with us. We were the weird church in our city and possibly one of the smallest in number and yet our names would land on the desk of key pastors who were running big organisations and big churches. Some even sent spies out to see what was going on because we were always tapping into the supernatural. As amazing as that was, I've come to realise there's a 'truer truth' that we are now walking out as sons. We cannot permanently stay in a place where we are sensitive to the atmosphere and do the best we can while being positioned in creation through signs, wonders and miracles so that we can say that God was here. Shouldn't we be seated with Him? Shouldn't we be operating with Him? In **Matthew 6:10** we read what Yeshua said, "Your kingdom come. Your will be done on earth as it is in heaven."

He won't just come through signs, miracles and wonders but through us arcing with understanding and with the knowledge that we have in who we are because of encounters. This will position us in the Realms of our Father. In His house are many dimensions and in that place we can arc together with our physical body which brings about a transformation in creation as we begin to arc, engage and go through the process of maturity.

While creation is waiting for the revealing of the sons of God to manifest so that it can come back to its original estate, there are living Beings that begin to appear and the sun is one of them. As it beholds us it can begin to release and radiate the true light that was spoken of in **Genesis 1** when Yahweh said, "Let there be light." He spoke this phrase, knowing that sons would be positioned to govern the lesser light that is mentioned in **Genesis 1:14**. When I read what Yahweh framed for us by writing this Scripture I see He had us in mind because we have a co-labouring relationship with Him. He wrote our testimony scroll together with us so that we could be positioned in creation, above the sun, in the light which Yahweh spoke, so that the sun can look at us who are emanating the glorious light which we live from, so that the sun, in its function, can release the light which brings about the ever increasing glory. The sun cannot do that if we're entangled in the earth's system and structure.

We could sit around and wait for God's glory to be displayed through the giftings but I've seen that the giftings do not carry the same weight as they did ten years ago. The anointings on people in ministry are not working quite the way as in the past. I honour those in the position of prophet but I've seen so many prophets having to repent for some of the things they've spoken out, either because the word hasn't been fulfilled or the total opposite happened to what they prophesied. There is a lot of confusion so we cannot be satisfied with living under the sun, in its corrupted and fallen state, waiting for God to move.

Creation is not waiting for that! When miracles, signs and wonders are evident in the Church, it's for the Church in order to bring it into maturity. It's not so that we can go to Church because we've had a bad week or we've done silly things we feel guilty about that we feel we need to go and repent at the altar for. The system is there so we can repeat the same thing week after week. Repentance is not saying sorry so that we can go home feeling better. This is ending because creation has put a demand on us saying it's time for sons to be revealed. The sun is waiting for us to be in our rightful position, in the light that was spoken of in Genesis, so that when we see each other, the sun is in its place of honour because of the government that we carry so it begins to release the light we are living in.

When we hear teachings presented to us we must remember that they are gates that we have to behold and go through. We will not receive everything on a golden platter so that we don't have to do any of our own searching. Scripture says that we must knock and the door will be opened, we must seek and we will find. We must behold the countenance of who we are so we can go through the truth and begin to see how it arcs together with us so we can release it into all of creation.

Ian initially spoke about the Twelve Plumblines of encounter or the Twelve Strands of encounter and many people were scared to engage through fear of being deceived and didn't want to go to a place where they would be outside of a union with Yahweh. On the other hand there were others who were doing silly things and becoming involved with things that were not positioned in the truth and engaged with parallel worlds. Through encounters Ian had started to teach on the Twelve Strands. When I was listening to him teach, my physical ears were listening and my physical eyes were beholding while my spirit was going through the process because of my honour towards Ian and the relationship I have with him, which gave me the access to begin to explore what was beyond that which was being said.

In **John 14:6** we read, "Jesus said to him, 'I am the way, the truth, and the life. No one comes to the Father except through Me.'" This means no one can encounter the Kingdom Realms without Yeshua, who is the New and Living Way.

In **Acts 17:28** we read, "For in Him we live and move and have our being, as also some of your own poets have said,

'For we are also His offspring.'" First we encounter the Way, the Truth and the Life and then we are positioned IN the Way, Truth and Life where we get to live, move and have our being within the Kingdom Realms. These are the first six strands of the plumbline of encounter.

In **Romans 14:17** we read, "For the kingdom of God is not eating and drinking, but righteousness and peace and joy in the Holy Spirit." These are three strands of encounter that begin to arc with the previous two sets.

In **Zechariah 7:9** we read, "Thus says the Lord of hosts: 'Execute true justice, show mercy and compassion everyone to his brother.'" This chapter also talks about administrating judgement.

These are the Twelve Strands of our encounter that we use to measure all other encounters by. Many people have asked the process by which I take an encounter and apply the Twelve Strands to it. I arc them together to make sure that the encounter I had is within position with Yeshua and my function within the government of what I carry in the Kingdom Realms and then from there into creation. *Each of these Twelve Strands of encounter are Beings*. I don't listen to a teaching once and then put it into the back of my memory. Knowledge needs the encounter to administrate things so we can be transformed in the knowledge that we heard that came from revelation, which came from a place of mystery which was unlocked from the secret chambers of Yahweh. We cannot be satisfied with the knowledge we have. It has to arc with an encounter.

While I was engaging – which is something we all do differently – I encountered four Beings that looked like three strands standing in front of me. They were moving back and forth and the colour of their countenance started to change as they were engaging with me. Through cardiognosis I knew that the first Being was composed of the *beit din* of the Way, the Truth and the Life and we started to echo into each other. The next Being was also engaging with me in the same frequency and same colours and this Being was made up of the three entities of Living, Moving and Have My Being. They also echoed in me and I in them. Righteousness and Joy and Peace who are Beings too in their *beit din* of three came and presented themselves to me as one Being.

These encounters took a few weeks to work through and I focused on figuring out who these individual Beings were so that I could be in the Way and the Truth and the Life, so that I could know them and they could know me through a mutual relationship. The Way is the path that makes up this Being which is engaging with us while arcing with Truth and Life, and the *beit din* engages with us through the three-in-one. Everything in the Kingdom is positioned strategically and nothing happens by accident. Yahweh, Yeshua and *Ruach haKodesh* are three-in-one. As people, we are three-in-one, spirit, soul and body. As I was engaging with these Beings I was reading the Scriptures, which are life if we go *through* them and sit *in* them. I love knowledge but it's pointless if it does not lead me into an encounter. If I have knowledge without encounter it will equip me to become more religious because I will place a ceiling above me if I believe I've seen the fulness of what a topic can give to me. That was the problem with the Pharisees in the days of Yeshua which is why He addressed them and said they only saw things from one perspective which was from a place of law, but that He was the true life and the way. They rejected Him because He didn't come in the form that they thought He should be in.

51

As I was engaging in the entanglement of the Way and the Truth and the Life, they were beginning to be in me and around me, engaging with my spirit-man through the eight gates that lead into my soul with the seven gates and into my physical body with the five gates, which is an echo chamber of an encounter that took place. When I walk in creation it releases a frequency of this encounter that I am living from a dimension we were always meant to live from and arcing together with **Genesis 1:1**. This is the theme I'm carrying at the moment which is 'let there be light.'

When I started to engage with the three-in-one Being of the Way, Truth and Life and began to understand their function within me and my function in arcing with them, this Being turned and introduced me to Live, Move and Have My Being. They arced together because this is a process of maturity and not just about having knowledge. This is about powerful knowledge *arcing* with an encounter which sets us in a place so we can begin to behold Beings within the Kingdom who want access to what we carry. As the various Beings began to engage with me here on earth and in my position with the Kingdom, I realised and understood that I live and move and have my being together with them. I am a spiritual being and they are spiritual Beings, who are the *beit din* sitting within the being I was having relationship with and getting to know, and they started to release life within me.

As I walked this encounter out with Live, Move and Have My Being, it turned and introduced me to Righteousness, Joy and Peace. When we engage with these Beings it changes everything. When I started to understand my function as a son with Righteousness, Joy and Peace I realised they wanted to engage with us because of the record of what we carry, having moved from a corrupted seed-line under the sun to undergo a transformation to end corruption, so that we can be part of turning creation back to its original intent. We are the ones steering this ship.

The first three Beings were now part of who I am as I was engaging with them and they began to turn together to introduce me to Justice, Judgment and Mercy. This is an incredible Being! When we understand our position and where we operate from, Justice, Judgement and Mercy carry such a transformation to creation when we operate with the other three-in-one Beings, because we start to think the way Yahweh thinks.

We have to be so careful when we see something within the earth without being in union with our Father and we haven't engaged in these Beings. If we make a judgement call on something it can be scary if we don't have the heart of Yahweh. Many times people will have undealt with issues and emotional things in their lives and when they see something they will go after it and make a judgment call without having our Father's heart on the matter. They think they're doing right but are causing more chaos because they aren't in union and relationship with the Way, the Truth and the Life, within in Him I Live, Move and Have My Being, and within Righteousness, Joy and Peace and finally Justice, Judgement and Mercy.

As I was engaging the four three-in-one Beings I realised that Yahweh was starting to reveal the upper and lower waters to me and how this function becomes like a mirror as mentioned in **1 Corinthians 13:12**. I was a son beginning to behold in order to reveal. When we see these Beings arcing together we notice that they take on the form of the letter *Shin*. Within my encounter, I started to understand what

Yahweh was saying. He said to me that I was the Tree of Life, positioned within creation and what I behold will begin to unfold, as a mirror, reflecting it into creation. Every part of these Beings started to behold their function within me, through an encounter, and as in a mirror I became an echo chamber in my position as a son, to bring into existence that relationship through union that I have with the Way, the Truth and the Life and all the other Beings.

The first three three-in-one Beings were operating in their own function of Faith, Hope, and Love who also looked like a three-in-one Being, shaped like the *Shin*. As Faith, Hope and Love arced together with the first four Beings, they created a menorah which is within us and creates the seven Realms of Heaven: The Kingdom of the Earth, the Kingdom of God, the Kingdom of Heaven, Heaven, Heaven of Heavens, Perfection and Eternity. This encounter allowed me to engage with four Beings who were in unison and union, arcing together with Faith, Hope and Love within the menorah which is positioned within us and arcing together with the seven Kingdoms, coming through the Door of First Love and engaging with our eight spiritual gates, which open to our seven spiritual gates, which open to the five gates to our physical body, emanating this light which Yahweh released when He said, "Let there be light," and when He saw us He saw that it was good. When He saw these encounters, He saw that it was good.

We must expect to transform our minds and behold the mystery in who we are because these Beings want to engage with us. We are able to have relationship with all of them. This is how we can judge an encounter through these Beings we are in relationship with.

Twelve Plumb-Lines

You can display the heart of Yahweh and who you are because you are functioning out of the 12 Plumb-Lines

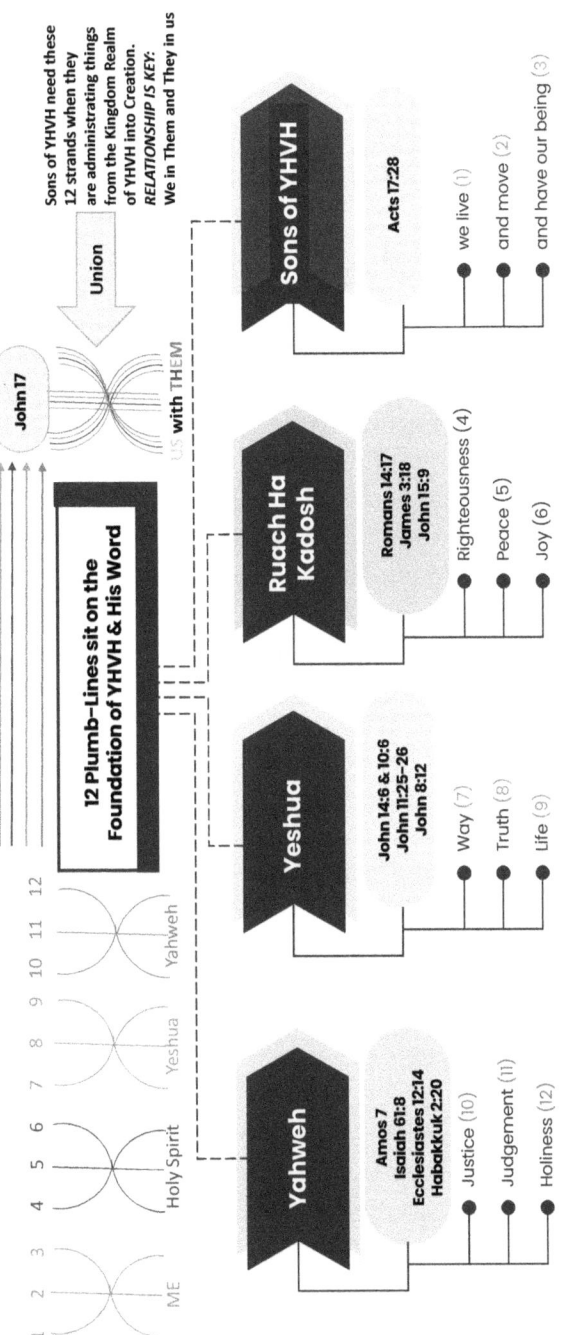

Sons of YHVH need these 12 strands when they are administrating things from the Kingdom Realm of YHVH into Creation. *RELATIONSHIP IS KEY:* We in Them and They in us

Union

John 17

US with THEM

12 Plumb-Lines sit on the Foundation of YHVH & His Word

Sons of YHVH

Acts 17:28

- we live (1)
- and move (2)
- and have our being (3)

Ruach Ha Kadosh

Romans 14:17
James 3:18
John 15:9

- Righteousness (4)
- Peace (5)
- Joy (6)

Yeshua

John 14:6 & 10:6
John 11:25-26
John 8:12

- Way (7)
- Truth (8)
- Life (9)

Yahweh

Amos 7
Isaiah 61:8
Ecclesiastes 12:14
Habakkuk 2:20

- Justice (10)
- Judgement (11)
- Holiness (12)

1 2 3 4 5 6 7 8 9 10 11 12

ME   Holy Spirit   Yeshua   Yahweh

Diagram by Vitor Ferrão

Chapter 4
Living An Ascended Life

To qualify the phrase 'we live an ascended life' I describe it like this. As we sleep on our bed at night engaging with our natural and carnal bodies, our spiritual body is the one which is seated in Christ in heavenly places, on our seat of rest, which is on our mountain of government. As we are seated in Christ we come into divine union and as we sleep we engage and go through the veil of His flesh which is the new and living way. This shows that we do not actually ascend, we are living an ascended life by being aware of where our other bodies are which all culminate in our god body. Many of us are not aware of our other bodies - terrestrial body, celestial body, and god body but as our carnal body sleeps our natural body, through our spirit-man and our soul, begins to arc with our spiritual body. The reason I don't like using the phrase 'let us ascend' is because I strongly believe in the power of words so when I say, "Let us ascend," I'm framing something with the breath of my mouth and saying that we have to claw our way up into something meaning that we're not already there. It's not about ascending but rather how to live an ascended life with our soul and spirit because we are ascended, regardless of whether we know it or not and regardless of whether we can feel it or not.

One night I was sleeping and my soul and spirit had a massive encounter where one of my natural bodies, my look-alike bodies, went somewhere and did something I was fully aware of. When I came into my consciousness and woke up, I wondered why I would even have thought or dreamt that? I absolutely knew that I had gone somewhere to do something. In order for me to talk about living an ascended life I want to address the issue of who we are.

Genesis 1:1 says,"In the beginning, God created the heavens and the earth."

The Hebrew version is this אלוהים את השמים ואת הארץ בראשית ברא - *B'resheet bara Elohim etz hashamaim v'etz haeretz.*

<u>In the beginning</u> - *B'resheet.*
This means the first, the principal thing of its kind. It doesn't mean at the beginning but in the beginning when the chief principal thing happened at this particular formation of time. This is the first of its kind. Do you know there are many other dimensions before The Beginning?

<u>Created</u> – *Bara.*
There was a shaping, a fashioning, a creating, and a birthing of something which was a first of its kind.

<u>Elohim</u>
Divine ones, or gods. Elohim is a plural word not singular.

B'resheet bara Elohim etz hashamaim: in the first place of the birthing, divine ones or gods created waters.

<u>Waters</u> – *shamaim.*
The waters or the heavens or the highest waters. There are two *Mems* in *shamaim*, the open *Mem* and the closed *Mem* representing the upper and the lower waters. The heavens are both the upper and lower waters, the highest ether where the celestial bodies revolve and move. The *Shin* in *shamaim* means

57

to pull apart in order to behold the upper and lower waters.
<u>Earth</u> – *Haeretz*.
The firm world or land.

Let's read this again: In the beginning (not at the beginning) the first place we were in, there was a birthing and a shaping by divine ones or gods to create the space where the celestials move in the upper and lower waters and the land.

How do we live an ascended life? We already were in a place of ascension so we just need an awareness of it and how to arc with *that* body. When we're sleeping we need to know how to arc with our celestial body, our terrestrial body as well as our spiritual body and to remember what they've done. We need to know which body is speaking to us through quantum entanglement - when one moves the other moves at the same time. If my terrestrial body is moving to and fro on the face of the earth and sees something, and stops to look, my carnal body notices that and tells me that it's feeling something but I'm not sure what it is. In the Church age, we didn't have a framework for this so we would say that the Holy Spirit brought something to our attention. Actually, because Holy Spirit has allowed it, my terrestrial body has seen something and through quantum entanglement this carnal body turns too and I know that I can feel or sense something. So now I look at my terrestrial body and ask it what it sees. From that place, I see what it sees and I begin to engage. I also do this with my spiritual body where I turn to it, seated in Christ in divine union by sharing breath, and I arc with it through the body and the blood of Yeshua haMashiach. We cannot do these things without Him. Also, Holy Spirit gives me permission and takes me into these realms because He is my guide and helps me as the *paracletos*.

We're always seated with Christ, not only when we're good, so we can arc with our two bodies because we were seated there in the beginning when gods or Elohim created the heavens (the upper and lower waters) and the land. We're not only arcing from here but also from the place where we've come from – we've just forgotten where that is. The key to living an ascended life is remembrance. We must remember who we are, where we are placed, who we are placed in, as well as knowing where we are now.

In the world of formation, where we form something with the breath of our mouth, creation happens. It's a formative process and everything that we are in the process of forming is pushed into manifestation. To get to this final phase is problematic because we don't remember where we come from and we don't remember what we did in that place. We have forgotten that we are a six-part being able to arc with our different bodies.

I've learned that I'm always present in that place and I can operate in the world of formation, through the process of what I'm doing, bringing it into creation thus causing manifestation. I don't have to claw myself to this place because I'm always there in Yahweh. While we're sitting here on earth in our carnal body, looking at others, we can send our natural bodies (which look like ourselves) to other places to preside over things that Yahweh has allowed us to preside over. I've done this many times before. As a younger Christian I would tell God that I wanted to feel my elbow touching Him and I'm really at that place now, through the divine imaginative process which is a place of formation, where I can literally feel my arm next to His because I'm in divine union with Him. I'm seated with Him in heavenly places and when I enter through the body and blood of Yeshua I can feel it. My carnal body can also feel it through quantum entanglement. This is an ascended life, understanding that it is right here next to us because the Kingdom is as close as the breath on our face.

Many people say they cannot see the power, they cannot see things being created but I'm telling you it's all around us. There is a wonderful testimony that has come out of Ukraine recently. A Christian base there, which has young people from all over the world in attendance, had run out of money and food, but every day they opened the store cupboard and the food was there again. That is power! We won't know how to make food until we're in a place of danger. The same thing happened in my city recently during an attempted coup. It was a crazy time of guns being fired and scary things happening but it was also a time where the door of the divine provision of the widow's oil opened through *Dalet*. It was exceptional! Every time I speak about this an Angelic being appears in the room. They love our testifying about the goodness of Yahweh.

In **John 17:21-24** we read the real Lord's prayer, not the prayer the Lord taught the disciples to pray, "That they all may be one, as You, Father, are in Me, and I in You; that they also may be one in Us, that the world may believe that You sent Me. And the glory which You gave Me I have given them, that they may be one just as We are one: I in them, and You in Me; that they may be made perfect in one, and that the world may know that You have sent Me, and have loved them as You have loved Me. Father, I desire that they also whom You gave Me may be with Me where I am, that they may behold My glory which You have given Me; for You loved Me before the foundation of the world. That they may be one Father as You are in Me and I am in You that they also may be one in Us, that the world may believe that You sent Me. And the glory which You gave Me I have given them."

As we live in Him the glory, He gave to Yeshua has been given to us. It is interesting that Yeshua wants us to be with Him where He is now. This speaks about a place inside of Himself, the hiddenness inside the cleft of the rock, even though we're on the earth. I love this prayer because He is talking about an ascended life.

In this place of ascension, it's not about us feeling good or spiritual so we can feel Yeshua but about being in the ninth day of creation where there is a new heaven and a new earth being created. We must move from the place of formation to the place of creation and then to the place of manifestation. This is what an ascended life does which is why we do not orgnise events to become ascended. We are ascended and living in an ascended life. As we keep repeating this the breath of our mouth begins to create a manifestation of truth. I am ascended. I'm living an ascended life. I'm arcing with my ascended self all the time so I don't need to have an event to ascend, as I'm always in that place.

When we begin to come into that place of manifestation we cannot create what we cannot see, so we have to go through the door of our imagination to be able to see in order to give birth to it so it can be manifest. We must go through this divine process of seeing something so we can form it and then manifest it into creation. This process constantly moves one within the other. We cannot birth what we haven't formed within ourselves. To give birth to something we need to go through a formation process. We see it and we speak it by sharing breath until it's created into reality.

In **Genesis 1** man was formed in the realms of formation by Yahweh's words. He knew what He wanted, formed it within Himself and all He had to do was breath it out. Man was then taken from that place of speaking it out and brought into reality. Yahweh, through formation, formed man by speaking him into existence through breath. After this global COVID-19 pandemic has eased off and restrictions are lifted we must be particularly cautious to not go back to the old ways. We don't want to look for the new normal because that does not fit in the process of formation. As one who is living an ascended life we MUST create new things. We do this by being in the world of formation. We see it then give birth to it and this process begins to create so we can bring it into manifestation through formation and through our breath to create new things in this present time and beyond.

Yeshua said, "Let them be with Me and see the glory." He was speaking while still on the earth but I believe He was also speaking about when He was going to be ascended and transfigured into His glorious body. He was saying let them be with Me because there's no distance between this world and the next.

The prayer that was taught to the disciples was, "our Father who art in this amazing, glorified place, *shamaim*, hallowed and glorious is Your name. Your Kingdom come, all that I see, I breathe in. Your will be done on the earth, and I release what I've seen. Give me today, as I sit in this place, my daily bread."

When I understood this from a Jewish perspective I learned that they took the hook that the priests used, which looked like the letter *Shin*, and hooked it into the daily meat offering giving them their daily meat supply. We now can receive our daily full supply of the mysteries and the secrets of Yahweh. Just what is needed for today. That's the prayer that Yeshua gave to the disciples and then said they must not be like the gentiles, pagans, Pharisees, and Sadducees who prayed repetitive prayers. What did we do? In school and in Church we made 'the LORD'S Prayer' a repetitive prayer!

When we live in this ascended life, how are we going to function in the area of formation, manifestation and breathing into creation? It's what we did in the beginning with Elohim. To be able to do this again we must pray in the Spirit *and* pray in tongues which takes us to a place of awareness – not to a place of ascension – but to an awareness of where we are seated in Christ. The Word has numerous examples:

Romans 8:26 we read, "Likewise the Spirit also helps in our weaknesses. For we do not know what we should pray for as we ought, but the Spirit Himself makes intercession for us with groanings which cannot be uttered." We must remember that the *Mem* hums and the *Shin* has a sssshh sound.

Ephesians 6:18 says, "praying always with all prayer and supplication in the Spirit, being watchful to this end with all perseverance and supplication for all the saints."

Jude 1:20 reads "But you, beloved, building yourselves up on your most holy faith, praying in the Holy Spirit."

1 Corinthians 14:13-15, "Therefore let him who speaks in a tongue pray that he may interpret. For if I pray in a tongue, my spirit prays, but my understanding is unfruitful. What is the conclusion then? I will pray with the spirit, and I will also pray with the understanding. I will sing with the spirit, and I will also sing with the understanding. "

John 4:24, "God is Spirit, and those who worship Him must worship in spirit and truth."

Romans 8:27, "Now He who searches the hearts knows what the mind of the Spirit is, because He makes intercession for the saints according to the will of God."

How do we begin to terraform? How do we begin to operate in this ascended life? How do we know that we're in an ascended life? By praying in the Spirit. Praying begins to awaken our carnal and natural body to remember that we can engage and arc with our spiritual body and then turn and look at ourselves. Someone said to me that they cannot see, so I told them to look at me, step out of their body, turn around and look at their body. They did so and by doing this were able to divide their soul and spirit. Just because we cannot see this with our natural eyes does not mean it's not there. It is. We need to start operating in this. We don't have to have an event to live an ascended life, we're already living it. We're always seated in Christ. Scripture doesn't say we're seated in Christ in heavenly places when we behave or when we're praying or when we're good. We are always seated there so we are always in an ascended life.

The way to stir it up is to pray in tongues, step through the veil of His flesh, arc with that body then turn and look at our terrestrial body which travels to and fro on the face of the earth and then we all turn to the celestial body which governs in the celestial arena with celestial beings. There will come a day when all of these bodies arc together and will take on the resurrected incorruptible Body. Yeshua's body changed in the tomb, demolecularised itself, and took on the resurrected body. My body is learning how to that. I speak it by framing it

64

with the breath of my mouth. I tell my body that it is learning how to demolecularise itself and bring itself into a god body so that I, like Enoch, can go up and down at will through portals into the realms of His Kingdom, operating there and coming back again and taking my body with me. If Enoch, Elijah, and John the Revelator can do it, I can do it too. That is why we can walk through walls.

When we speak in tongues and engage with the mysteries we have to speak it into creation with intentionality. We cannot speak in tongues while our mind is busy with other things. This is unfruitful because our mind does not understand but our spirit does. We must engage the carnal and natural body. Our spirit and soul need to engage while we pray in tongues and once we've opened a pathway between the two it's not hard to find again as it always stays open.

Sonship makes what we create, harmonious. As a son, we never do something that is completely out of our family agreement. We uphold the family name. I am passionate about family dynasty and as we create family dynasty within the Masters and Nieuwenhuis households we know that our children and their children will always work together to further our dynasty because we uphold the Master's name and the Nieuwenhuis name. We also uphold the name of the tribe we walk with so we don't engage with crazy stuff because we carry the name. When sons, who carry His name, are living in this ascended place and begin to create, it becomes harmonious.

When we create outside of sonship and move away from our place in Him we start to create idols and things that are after our own heart. Once we've created idols we take them into the world with us and we wonder why there is chaos around us and we get mad with people because things don't work. This is a result of us making idols according to what is inside of us outside of sonship. Whole ministries can collapse because they've been built on the idols in the hearts of man. They saw and birthed something that was not in the heart of God.

When we have a God-idea and the desire of our heart is being fulfilled through our destiny scroll, what we create sits within sonship, lordship, and kingship because we're in an ascended life. We remember we were in the first place of the birthing and the shaping as a divine one, with Him, creating the celestial beings AND the upper and the lower waters and *terra ferma*. We remember who we are. Then in the new covenant, we remember that we are in Him and the glory that has been given to us. Through our mouth we begin the process of formation so we can create something in order to bring it into manifestation. We give birth to what we see in the place of formation by our breath and walking together in sonship with all those whom Yahweh has given us and we begin to create new things in 2022 through sonship, lordship, and kingship thereby creating a harmonious future. We don't walk into the place of idols because we've gone through the process of living an ascended life.

When my husband transitioned, our ministry lost one person. He left because he was an orphan and had found a father-figure in my husband, so when my husband died, this man felt so let down by another father-figure that he walked away. Apart from him, we lost no one and the numbers grew and grew. As the seed died it was manifested in formation and creation in a few of his sons, one of whom is Rick. I saw the mantle come on several people and begin to rise. I know that if we transitioned into glory now or began to do things like Enoch and travel up and down that there would be others who would be able to stand with this tribe because this is birthed out of sonship, lordship, and kingship and creating a harmonious future. It is also not an idol.

Someone once told me that they could run this ministry much better than me so I gave them the keys to my house and my car and told them she could have the whole Hub movement. The reason I was able to respond in this way is because I'm a son. I don't have to panic about anything and I don't have to be concerned about Church or Movement splits because I'm operating from a place of sonship, lordship and kingship, living in an ascended life. Because I know who I am, I am creating harmony and not idols. I am not defined by the Hubs or the Nest or the Flight School or even Ian Clayton. I am defined by being a son because the Father leant over me and looked at me and asked me, "Son, what do you want?" He thought I looked like Yeshua, like the Elohim. Even if the Hubs fell apart tomorrow, I'm so defined by Yeshua and hidden in Him and have become one with Him that it wouldn't matter. I know who I am because I'm in an ascended position all the time. I do not wake up in the morning wondering where I am and what I'm supposed to be doing because it's an all-consuming process. I wake up from dreams and start analysing whether I was in my natural body or in a dream state. If it was a dream, was it an encounter or was it in the spirit-realm? Was it in the future or is it in the present? I go through the whole process and then go back to sleep.

We live an ascended life by breath. The breath of the words we speak and pray do create and form and once they are spoken out they land and they manifest which is why we need to be careful with what we say. I've dealt with my junk and have stopped listening to the little demons that hang around rejection. I will not drink from the well of rejection so I don't create new demons. I've cast them out twice already. I've now learned how to overcome.

We live an ascended life by loving our bodies. I cannot walk through walls yet, but I can see through the wall to the other side. The first time this happened I was in Norway and could see an entity on the other side of the wall that had been sent to harass us. I didn't have to open the curtains or the door in order to see it. I engaged with it and asked it what it wanted. It told me the reason and I told it to leave. It was so scared of me! In order to walk through a wall, we have to honour our body so we can take it through the wall. So, living an ascended life, the life that goes to and fro on the face of the earth and like Enoch, walking with our god-body wherever we go, means we must realise that our body is the temple of the Holy Spirit. Society has told us there is no good thing in the flesh and we haven't learned to love the process of our temple, the temple of the divine, the temple of the Holy One so that we can take it and walk through a wall. We must undo all the negative things we were told during childhood. We might have been told we were too fat or too thin, too short or too tall, etc.

We live an ascended life through the Word and the living letters. The Word became flesh and dwelt among us.

We also live an ascended life by being thoroughly wrapped up in the Blood of the Lamb. The speaking Blood is so important. There was a time when many folks were engaging with the wrong things and so I encouraged them to ask certain questions when they encountered various beings; things like, "Who are you? Who is Jesus to you? What is the

Blood to you?" If the being embraced the Blood of the Lamb, that was fine. If not, they needed to leave it alone and not engage at all.

Anything outside of the Blood is outside of Christ and still carries a record of ourselves, our DNA and sin. Whatever sphere we go into will then have a repeated pattern of our DNA. As a result, we have a seed-line coming down in our genetics which speaks because the genetics outside of the Blood still carry a record of itself and of its sin to every sphere it operates in. That is why we have to deal with our cellular memory which is the sphere outside of the Blood which is speaking. We need to make sure that we are constantly in the place of understanding that living an ascended life means we need to go through the Blood of the Lamb and we engage with our other bodies. We drink His Blood. He said we must remember Him as we drink the Blood. **John 6:53-57.**

Emanation means something that emanates from a particular source. So a Being or a force which is a manifestation of God means its emanation comes from God. You and I and the emanation of who we are in Him, begin to emanate the glory. When we go somewhere, the Blood speaks first. When we live in an ascended we must always remember the Blood which is why when we have breaking of bread we drink the speaking Blood and eat the flesh, which is the death and the resurrected body. That begins to emanate from within me which comes from the source which is Christ in me and I become a being or a force which becomes a manifestation of God because I'm living an ascended life.

If we keep saying that we want to ascend or we want to have an ascending time with a group or have an ascension prayer, then the words of our mouth will keep us under the sun. If, however, we change our wording and the breath of our mouth says we want to engage because we're in an ascended lifestyle and we arc with all six bodies and with Yahweh and the Courts of Heaven then we step through the veil of His flesh and remember and arc with our other bodies and immediately the realms of the Kingdom are around us, in us and through us.

That is why we can draw the menorah in our body which shows the Kingdom of the Earth, the Kingdom of God, the Kingdom of Heaven, Heaven, Heaven of Heavens, Perfection and Eternity. On the same menorah, which is a wheel within a wheel, we can draw the different courts of heaven. We can also draw the cube of our life which sits within us and is comprised of the natural and carnal bodies, the spiritual body and our terrestrial body which culminate in a god-body which then emanates outwards.

Our whole body can step through into the Kingdom and we can engage through our spiritual points into the *choshek* and into the realms of His Kingdom and we can access our daily bread and our bodies arc together all the time. All of this is done through the Blood when we understand that we live an ascended life. Instead of saying, "Let's do an ascension," let us rather say, "We'll come together, go through the Blood of the Lamb, go through the veil of His flesh, arc with our bodies, and breathe Him in." We must remember where we are, where we are situated and who we belong to. We must remember that the glory in Him is the glory in us. Then we can engage because we remember what we have to do. We're not ascending into it, because we're in an ascended state all the time. Every day, when we're sleeping and when we're awake, day in and day out, we're always in an ascended state from within ourselves.

We want to know God as He was in the beginning when He created the heavens and the earth. We want to know Him and to walk in divine union with Him in the ascended life of who we are, in our god-body, always before the throne of Yahweh. In order to know God, we must know "no thing." We have to overcome our image of God. We also have to overcome our image of where we are sitting. If we have an image of what God looks like or an image of heaven or an image of what we look like we will never live an ascended life. We must know no thing because God sits in a place of nothing. Scripture says nothing is impossible for God – no thing. This means He knows no thing. There is nothing before Him or after Him. He's all in all so when the Word says nothing is impossible for God, all in all is possible because there is no thing in Him – He's the beginning and the end and everything in between.

I want to say that we must know no thing of what we look like in the realms of the Kingdom. We must know nothing, no thing, with regards to what it looks like to be in an ascended life. We must take this, breathe it in and keep on framing it with the words of our mouth so that we become aware of where we are constantly seated and it is in this place that we are going to begin to change this *terra ferma*, where the place of formation will become the manifestation of a new heaven and a new earth. We must get rid of our image of God as an old and angry Being who does strange things. God is complete. He is a pure Spirit. Those who worship Him must worship Him in Spirit and in truth. In Him is no thing and the only image He allows for Himself, is His Son. Dr Ogbonnaya says, "He manifested Himself on the face of the earth through a Son who was willing to give up His identity and image to make His Father glorified." Yeshua said that if we have seen Him we have seen the Father.

71

When we say that we are seated with Christ in an ascended place we breath Him in and see no thing except Him and He sees no thing but us and there is constant synergy. We look like Him, He looks like us. From that place we can begin to breath into creation and create whatever we want to because we only do the will of our Father. We've given up the right to think of what God looks like and the right to know what we think He wants. We see no thing except Him and then we hear what He has to say. No one knows the thoughts of God except the Spirit of God but here was Lucifer who sat in that place above the throne of God and had one of the highest positions over the Father. He had all the timbrels and musical instruments within his body and he was music in heaven. He saw everything that God was creating and one day he said that he knew the mind of God, how He thought and how He created and said he would exalt himself above the knowledge of God and he began to exalt himself above the mind of God. The Bible says no one knows the mind of God except the Spirit of God, **1 Corinthians 2:11**. In that place of knowing, Lucifer created idols. The book of Enoch says that the people were taught how to kill a baby in the womb, how to go engage in warfare and how to use pharmakeia for healing the body. The men did things with animals and fish and birds and began to mix seed. Some of the nephilim race began to create beings that were not in God's heart which resulted in twelve-foot men of renown who resorted to cannibalism when they couldn't be given enough food to sustain them. I believe the dinosaur and Neanderthal ages were part of these idols which were created in the heart of Lucifer and ha'satan because they were not operating out of sonship. You and I operate out of a place of sonship.

Angels have a will and within himself Lucifer said he knew

what God was thinking and he believed he knew the mind of God. He wasn't in the place of no thing. He decided he knew and then proceeded to exalt himself above it. If he stayed in the place of no thing, he would have realised it would never happen. God has said there is no redemption for the angels and the sons of God and those beings who have fallen. In the book of Enoch they asked Enoch to go and plead their case because they were so sorry and couldn't even look at heaven. God said there was no redemption because He had told them they couldn't create because they were themselves created beings and not made in His image. They were created to worship only God. They had one function but they came out of that place of no thing and began to teach the people. God said that the things the people were taught by them were useless and that they didn't know what He was thinking. The things they thought God was doing were not done correctly by them and it brought destruction to the earth. God also said that the people had been taught to read and to write and that they would be cursed with it for the rest of their lives. The higher form of communication was engaging with the paleo and the Living Letters through cardiognosis and breathing life and emanating from within ourselves. We lost that because we thought we knew better. We need to be in that place where we know that in Him we have overcome our image of God and what we think He wants and how He thinks. There is no thing in us but to know Christ so we can immerse ourselves in Him while He immerses Himself into us and in that place emanation begins to happen and we live the ascended life in the place of formation, creation and manifestation. We will live the god-life, the divine ones that co-created right in the beginning and we will manifest here on *terra ferma* and begin to create today and beyond.

Chapter 5
The Power Of Breath

It's such a joy to see the mystery of what Yahweh is revealing in us as we strategically arc together upon the face of the earth and behold this truth that we are walking out, this mandate and scroll which creation is longing for. As we behold these teachings about the Kingdom and arc with them from our mountains, the Beings that live in the Kingdom Realms start coming to see what we are doing because of the frequency that is released. As we speak, they turn to encounter what is taking place in our lives because they want us to know who they are and they want us to be part of their journey as they are part of ours.

The power of breath has been fascinating for me. I've been speaking a lot from Genesis because there is so much within that portion of the Scriptures that begins to produce life. Yahweh created Adam in His image and then in **Genesis 2** He breathed the breath of life into Adam. At that moment, he was brought into Yahweh. When Yahweh breathed into Adam, he breathed in that breath and was filled with life. Adam understood who he was in creation and who he was as a spirit being. When Yahweh breathed the breath of life, Spirit to spirit, Adam took the breath and began to breathe. This exchange of breath released life. This life was far more than I think we realise. The life that Yahweh breathed into Adam is not the same life that we refer to today. We think life means to just be alive on the earth but there is something quite fascinating about that word 'life' and especially the breath of life.

I was at a conference where Ian was teaching, I was beholding and engaging with what I was hearing and what was being revealed because I wanted it. Ian told us about an encounter he had where Yahweh asked him if he lived to breathe or if he breathed to live. That statement sounds simple, but Ian does not make simple statements and there is such a depth here if we choose to behold what it truly means.

I began to ponder on and engage with this statement and what it meant to me. I remember driving and asking Yahweh, "Do I live to breathe? Or do I breathe to live?" I was trying to come to grips with the framework we have been taught, under the sun and in corruption, that the reason we breathe is to just sustain having life. I was pondering on the idea that we can breathe to begin to behold and reveal some things that are happening within the Kingdom Realms because of our engagement Spirit to spirit.

I thoroughly enjoy freediving. In a nutshell, freediving is being placed in a relatively deep and large body of water. You take one breath on the surface and begin to descend into the depths of the ocean, holding that one breath. There are no oxygen tanks for you to take a quick breath if you need one. As a free-diver you begin to learn to engage with and govern your body so that your heart rate slows down. The lower beats per minute allow you to hold your breath for longer. As a free-diver (which is useful when spearfishing), you want to hold your breath for as long as possible. The longer you hold your breath, the lower your heart rate drops, the deeper you can dive and the more time you get to spend under the water. As a free-diver there are certain techniques that you need to practice and engage with, one of them being the breath hold. It's interesting to find out how long we can hold our breath for! We have to train our mind to know that it's okay for our body to be without oxygen for a period of time before we blackout.

One evening I had been pondering on whether I breathe to live or live to breathe as I was getting ready to do the breath hold technique exercise. To prepare for that there are certain breaths that you take which start to lower your heart rate. I aim at around 44 to 48 beats per minute before I am ready to take that one breath which will allow me to go to the depth I need to go. I was watching my heart rate monitor and engaging with my body until I got my heart rate down sufficiently where I was ready to take in that last breath. As I took it, there was something different about it. At first, I wondered where it had come from because it wasn't my normal breath that I take, but I had now breathed it in and was holding it all the while thinking that something was different.

I started my stopwatch to help me calculate how long I needed to hold my breath for as this is part of my exercise. As I held my breath, I closed my eyes and engaged with my heart to make sure it stayed at low beats per minute. During that time, I was also in touch with my body, but this exercise was different because every beat of my heart began to release atoms that were releasing life into every fibre of my being. With every beat of my heart, I could see the life and feel it and I started to wonder where I was. My body started to feel different, yet I was fully aware and conscious that I was holding my breath. This unfolded for a little while and I can remember enjoying this and engaging face-to-face with Yahweh, where I was spiritually breathing with Him and holding that one breath that I had taken.

After a while, I thought to myself that some time had already passed but I had no urge to breathe. My eyes were open and I could feel the breath that I was holding but I didn't want to look at my stopwatch yet because I knew the moment I looked at it my mind would start releasing that urge to breathe. I left it a little while longer and just enjoyed the space I was in. Eventually I picked up my stopwatch and glanced at it. I was amazed! The time that I held that breath was double my personal best time! When my eyes looked at the numbers on my stopwatch and saw the time-lapse, my mind released a caution which triggered an urgency within my body to take in deep breaths. I was frantically trying to organize my thoughts into understanding what had just happened. In that moment the voice of Yahweh said this, "Son, haven't you been asking the question, 'Do you live to breathe or do you breathe to live?' Son, when you breathe the breath that I breathed into your spirit-man, that breath was never meant to sustain life. It was meant to create life."

Because of my engagement in beholding what the mystery of breath means I believe that I took a breath of air and in an encounter, face to face with Yahweh, breathing spirit to Spirit, His breath released life to me. My physical body did not need the breath I breathed in creation because it now understood the function of breath. That breath was no longer needed to sustain life but was designed to create life.

After that encounter, I started to behold what happened in Adam after Yahweh breathed the breath of life into him, as recorded in **Genesis 2**. Through that breath, Yahweh had given Adam the function and administration to create. Adam was the one who began to name creation and give details of their description because he had the breath of life. We are on a journey of beginning to understand, through knowledge, because of an encounter, that we were created from the very beginning, in the image of Yahweh and the breath that we should be breathing is from a different realm, which comes when we are face to face with Yahweh. This breath gives us the capacity to create life from within us as we speak and frame the breath of Yahweh. The breath of Yahweh is not for sustaining our physical body and life here in creation, but its function is for us to create life.

If we, in this journey, begin to behold this truth and we sit in a place of engaging with the transfiguration that our physical bodies are going through, could it be possible that in time to come we won't need to breathe the breath of creation to sustain life? We would be positioned face to face with Yahweh where that breath creates within us the breath to create.

Paul addressed the subject of death in the Scriptures and wrote, "O Death, where is your sting? O Hades, where is your victory?" Could he have been talking about a generation that won't be within the system and the structure of the earth where we get our source of life from? Could it be that he was talking about a day where sons will go in through Yeshua, the New and Living Way, to engage spirit to Spirit because we understand, through the knowledge of what we've been taught and through encounters, that we can be face to face with Yahweh? We can just read Scripture and enjoy it but feel that it's way too much work to apply it to our own lives, or we can begin to stand out by modelling, framing and speaking what we've experienced through a personal encounter.

After my encounter, I was completely undone! It wasn't just about holding one breath and doubling my personal best time because that's irrelevant to the subject I'm addressing now. Yahweh took the breathing technique that I was using and allowed me to arc together with Him so that when I took that breath it wasn't within creation, but I took it face-to-face with Yahweh. Whenever I practiced my breathing techniques, I would imagine that I was breathing in Yahweh's breath. It just helped me to lower my heart rate and allowed me to be positioned on the seat of rest where my body could begin to feel the vibration of the breath I had just taken. Some people would call it a trance.

There are so many people that try and do this by faith but their unrenewed mind begins to war against the practical demonstrations that one must do to get into that place of beholding the truth. When Lindi was demonstrating how to breathe she breathed in for five seconds, held her breath for one second and let her breath out for four, which is the *Dalet*, into creation. She did this strategically for us. We can't just do it for the three minutes that Lindi did it at the conference and then say we didn't feel anything and we don't think it's working. Lindi taught us something in a few minutes that has become a lifestyle for her. The things that Yahweh has revealed to me have become possible because of my lifestyle of pursuit. I'm breathing it and I'm living it.

When I meet someone who has heard one of my teachings or has read one of my books, I often realize that they have preconceived ideas on how I received that revelation. I was having a conversation with someone and he started telling me some of the practices he was now doing and engaging with to obtain the mystery that I had received. I hadn't done a fraction of what he was doing and I wondered to myself whether I should tell him. His heart was in the right place, but as amazing as those practices and protocols were it is ultimately about a union and a relationship. I don't talk about everything that my Father and I are engaging with because the majority of it is for me. It is through the fruit of that encounter that I'll begin to speak about some of the transformation that's taken place within my life.

A major key for us is to engage who we were before the foundation of the earth, by going back to the place where we engaged the heart of Yahweh as a spirit being, coming face to face with Him and writing the scroll that we said yes to. We came into the existence of creation with that mandate. We are all aware that we have traded into concepts and ideas that have warred against the truth of who we are within the process of living life on earth, which is under the sun in corruption and going from bondage to decay.

There are sons that have stood at that place and have seen issues in some of the beliefs that the Church has had and we are now taking a stand and measuring them through the Twelve Strands, or the plumblines, of our encounter. They are Beings that are in relationship with us. During my encounter with these Beings, I found myself entangled within the Twelve Strands which were within me. Everything is positioned inside of us because we are the arc, we are the temple, we are the dwelling place of the fullness of the Kingdom here in creation.

I've been engaging with my spirit-man and beholding him because he is me. As I've walked this process out, I've also been beholding and engaging my soul, which is a being and is also me. I am also engaging with my physical body that we can all see. I'm persistent in this because I want my physical body to take on the reflection of what my spirit-man is engaging with. This is my journey and I won't easily share what happens between Yahweh and me in my quiet place. We all need to get our own revelation and engage with our own life with Yahweh so that it can become food for us as well as a testimony.

I'm fully aware that we're in creation where there is bondage and corruption and that the frequency which emanates from the sun is the frequency of chaos, but when we get to be in that place of government the sun will begin to behold that light that we are positioned in, which will be released through the union and the arcing of who we are. That light will bring about the frequency of transformation, bringing creation back to its original intent. It is our function and purpose to do that!

After the encounter that I had when I took that breath, I realized that my physical body was so content, it was so at peace that it no longer needed the breath of creation to sustain life in me. Every cell in my body responded by saying, "I remember this!" My lungs took on a different function and I felt that my physical body had positioned itself as a chamber and was telling me to release the life that I was now breathing as I was face to face with Yahweh. Before I could do that, I decided to see how long I had been holding my breath for. My body and mind both got a fright when they saw how much time had passed but my spirit-man was frustrated because I had almost achieved my goal.

I'm constantly expanding my spirit-man because of what we've been taught by the law and what is intertwined within the Earth's system and structure that we have become a slave to. I'm now untangling my belief system, through an encounter, even though I'm still present within creation and expanding my spirit-man, so that it begins to go through my soul and through my physical body, so it can be positioned outside of my body with my soul in the centre of my spirit, and my physical being in the centre of that, because that is the way we were designed by the breath of Yahweh right at the beginning.

I believe that when we do this process, even if it's by faith, creation begins to turn because it's seen us within our rightful position and our rightful place of government. Creation begins to yearn because we are the connection point and transition point from the Kingdom of Yahweh in us. We are the *Vav* hooked as an anchor within creation. We begin to behold what we are carrying within creation and creation begins to behold that truth and what we're living out.

That anchor point is so key. The function of an anchor is to lock in so that when you are locked in, although the current may be moving, although the waves might be there, the anchor allows you to lock your vessel in a particular spot so that you do not move. You're steadfast, you're staying focused, and you are where you need to be. We are the *Vav*, hooking into creation through who we are and the union that we have with Yahweh, through the breath, interlocking and engaging face to face with Yahweh, beholding and sharing His breath so that our physical body steps into its rightful position. As the *Vav* we begin to create and release life that comes from the source of where we live from.

In **John 20:19-22** we read, "Then, the same day at evening, being the first day of the week, when the doors were shut where the disciples were assembled, for fear of the Jews, Jesus came and stood in the midst, and said to them, 'Peace be with you.' When He had said this, He showed them His hands and His side. Then the disciples were glad when they saw the Lord. So, Jesus said to them again, 'Peace to you! As the Father has sent Me, I also send you.' And when He had said this, He breathed on them, and said to them, 'Receive the

Holy Spirit."'

There are only two times within the Scriptures that the breath that He breathes is mentioned. The first one is in **Genesis 2** when Yahweh breathed the breath of life into Adam and Adam began to take that breath within Yahweh. They were in complete union, and he took the breath from his Father and that became life to him that gave him the capacity to release life. The very next Scripture where that breath is mentioned is in **John 20:22** when Yeshua came into the room and said, "Peace be with you," and He began to show them who He was. He then breathed over them and said, "Now receive Holy Spirit".

In **Genesis 1** the Spirit of Yahweh was hovering and vibrating over the surface of the deep. That vibration began to release a frequency that began to do something to the waters and attracted the water's frequency to itself. Yeshua now breathed the breath that was breathed in Him by Yahweh. When Yeshua was on the cross and breathed out His last breath, it got dark. It wasn't the demonic spirits doing warfare, which is what the church has taught us, but it was Yahweh coming into that place. With Yahweh being there the sun lost its light because He was there in His fullness. The breath that Yeshua breathed out, Yahweh breathed in and that was when His body could not die, even though His body was lifeless on the cross, His body could not die because Yahweh and Yeshua were in union.

His physical body was taken to the tomb and was prepared for burial because of the religious process that needed to be fulfilled, but it was the breath that had been exchanged that gave life. Although His body was lying in that tomb, it had never died but was sitting in that place to behold that breath once again, to bring life. We know the tomb opened and Yeshua walked out. He was completely transfigured so that Mary could not recognize Him.

It is now our turn to step into that breath because our physical bodies are wanting to remember why we breathe. Our physical bodies want to remind us that there is a far greater capacity for life that we haven't yet touched. Life is not just having a good time in creation or setting up investments, although that is needed, but that's not life until we have breathed the breath of life, spirit to Spirit. This is the reason why I'm starting to understand what breath means and I'm continuously beholding the breath of Yahweh because if we behold the breath of Yahweh, spirit to Spirit, we are being recalibrated back into our original intent and our physical bodies are starting to take on the image of what our spirit-man is beginning to behold. When we engage with the breath and behold it, it transforms us.

We must get to the place of understanding that the breath we breathe was designed to create. We must get there through the power of knowledge and through encounter and until we do that, we still need the breath in creation to sustain us because of the law that our physical bodies have locked into. That however is not the end result for us, because we are navigating through processes and encounters, beginning to behold and understand the framework. We are going to places, where not many have gone, to begin to get answers for our physical bodies because if there is no one on the face of the earth who will model it, we aren't going to have the framework of that within creation, and we won't be able to see it evident. Are we getting persecuted for the things we talk about? Yes! I don't understand it because how can people not see and believe? How can people challenge me on this because there's so much life when I'm speaking to them?

When we arc things together something begins to materialize and through personal study, I've realized that this is connected to science as well as to our spiritual encounters, and we start seeing the fruit because of our union with Yahweh. It is energy that engages with light which creates matter. Our energy, which is a combustion of frequency in terms of engaging face to face with Yahweh, with that breath that we are breathing out and breathing in, is creating that energy that arcs together with created light. In the beginning, Yahweh spoke and framed light and said, "Let there be light" and there was light. Those two arcing together with who we are as sons creates matter.

There was a time when I relied on the gift of healing and I saw some incredible signs, wonders and miracles that happened because of the gift on my life. But that gift of healing that was resting upon me did not require maturity. It just required an acknowledgement of the gift on me for it to work. What I'm beginning to realise is that with us understanding that we were there before the foundation of the earth, when Yahweh said, "Let there be light," and now understanding that we are operating from that superior light, where there is no corruption, and now we are in creation, could it be possible that in time, if we do this correctly through the union that we have with Yahweh, that by the energy of our frequency arcing together with the created light, we will have the capacity to annihilate any corrupted seed-line that would be able to do away with sickness because we have given people the opportunity to live in health?

Do you think that Yeshua operated in that atmosphere? He did not need the gifts! So, how did He begin to release the fullness of the Kingdom that was within Him, into creation? He was operating from a superior light, the very one that Yahweh spoke from the very beginning that was within Him. If we can gain knowledge within that light and begin to behold our spirit-man where that light sits and begin to honour and arc and go through the process, we could allow that light to emanate, through the frequency of who we are in creation, where we can do away with the corrupted seed-line on the face of the earth. Then, in time to come, it is possible that there will no longer be sickness, but there will be an opportunity for people to behold the place of health.

I believe this is the promise of Yeshua when He said that we will do what He has done and greater works too. Decisions and choices were made further within the future of that statement where the gift was required because so many chose not to believe. The gifting was then given to the Church at its immaturity to hopefully bring them into a place of maturity.

The breath and the union that we have with Yahweh also transforms our thoughts and our mind. A transformed mind begins to engage with the physical body and what it once thought was impossible, now becomes possible. If I go back to some of the things that I heard Ian speak about in 2012, all of that was impossible. It was foolishness to the immature and religious Christian that I was, but now I'm gaining knowledge, I'm pursuing, I'm beholding and I'm seeing the maturity taking place within my life. Where what was once something that was completely impossible has now become logical and I'm going after the knowledge and the understanding, and I'm arcing with an encounter which allows me to see the fruit in my life.

Thought is so important and Yeshua obviously addressed

the thought life when He was engaging, walking and demonstrating what it looks like to be a son within creation. I remember going into a room within my mind when I was engaging with **Romans 12**, which talks about how we are not to conform any longer to the patterns of this world, but be transformed by the renewing of our mind, because only then will we be able to test and approve the will of God, His good, pleasing and perfect will. I then realized that I had so many strong beliefs that were religious in nature and that religiosity was warring against who I needed to be as a son. One day I was engaging with Yahweh and asking how does one renew the mind? Paul says we must renew it but how do I renew it?

I then found myself going into my own mind where I saw a door. Yahweh allowed me to go through the door and I found myself in a chamber called the subconscious. Within this chamber I saw old machinery which was ticking over. I didn't know what I was looking at and when I asked Yahweh, He said, "Son, this is your subconscious."

Yahweh told me that if I wanted to renew my mind then I would have to renew my subconscious. The problem is that we are hearing things that are bringing life to our spirit-man, but when we don't sit on it and engage within the process and the opportunity that we have been given, through the revelation and the mystery from a son that's presenting his life and his mountain to us. A week or two will pass and the subconscious will begin to tick over again and the revelation that had an opportunity to present life to us fades away. This is because the subconscious takes over in its old pattern and that mystery which came to us, to give us an opportunity to behold and engage becomes so foreign because your subconscious says, "What do you mean there's no such thing as a rapture?"

Our mind frames the subconscious of what we once believed and within the religious sense, the subconscious allows us to get into a groove where it requires us not to do anything because we're in a comfortable place and we just allow that motion to happen. As a son, it requires us to think differently, to engage differently, and to deal with belief systems that have warred against the knowledge of who we are as a son. So, the subconscious is a vital key because it wants to be renewed. When the subconscious is renewed there is a new thought process that begins to develop within us so that our mind can arc together to believe and see things that are possible and it becomes logical, so we can see it evident within our life as a son.

Even within creation, like physical sports, someone will need to push the limits to show the earth that is possible, and within that same week there are ten others doing what was once impossible. When the system says it's impossible, we only need one person who will go beyond their capacity to prove to themselves and the world that it is possible. This is why we are engaging, stepping in and beholding. I believe that we are the species, we are the tribe, we are the people in union that Yahweh has instilled within us the secrets to display a Kingdom that has not yet been displayed. We are in the forefront of this which means we are going to come up against things that people are upset about, and they want to persecute what we are talking about. At the end of the day, if we stand firm, engage and behold, we will set a pathway that will produce life that is engaging with the breath, face to face with Yahweh, so we can become like Him. That's what Moshe did when he went up the mountain. It wasn't a physical mountain as we know. It was the mountain of Yahweh and within that mountain were different realms that Moshe began to walk up and engage and behold. When he got to the top and he went into the mountain he began to engage Yahweh face to face. He began to breathe the breath of Yahweh as Yahweh breathed out and Moshe breathed in. He became the very image of the One that he was engaging with.

When Moshe came out the mountain and presented himself to the Israelites they were terrified because he had taken on the countenance of Yahweh through the breath of Yahweh. It's the breath that transforms. It's the breath that does not sustain life but produces life. When we breathe the breath of Yahweh, our physical body will not need the breath in creation. We are positioned within creation and that breath that we use is to behold and create what needs to be created within our area of influence and the arena that we operate from to release life. I can tell you about one person that I know, who I have been beholding and engaging with, who understands this process of engaging and beholding the breath of Yahweh in order to create. His name is Solomon.

Chapter 6
Engaging The Tutors And Governors

When Ricky and I work together, an arcing seems to take place between us which opens the Faces of the Deep and the gateways of Heaven! We are creating an inheritance and a dynasty. Holy Spirit told me to teach on the many different types of Governors and Tutors because over the last fifteen years we've come out of one truth and into another truth. We don't always have guidelines on what this looks like, how we should proceed, who they are, where they're from and what they do. We need to ensure that we engage with them in the proper manner and not get involved with familiar spirits.

I had been in ministry in the Charismatic Church as a pastor for twenty-five years when my husband transitioned. We had always been told, that as Christians, we don't speak to dead people. We know that Jesus died. He was a dead person who was raised from the dead but apparently that doesn't fit into the same category! We were also warned against talking to angels in case we were deceived. We were, however, allowed to talk to as many demons as we liked! We woke up in the morning and bound the devil and the demons, which I find interesting because Jesus died on the cross and He did all of that for us. When we start engaging with demons and giving breath to them, we create life in them and in so doing, we create our own demons. We don't want to create the demonic realm around us because it's already been defeated.

A demon once ran into my room in Guildford, England. It was bounding towards me on all fours so I kicked it and it rolled out the room yelping like a little dog. I told someone what had happened and he asked me what I had done to allow the demon into my house. I don't think like that and told him that demon had entered the wrong house and I kicked it right out! I don't talk to them, I don't engage with them and I don't ask them their name because I couldn't care less. Their father, the devil, is a liar, would they tell me the truth? They'll tell me whatever I want to hear to keep me busy for as long as possible, so I don't talk to them. I still see them sometimes but now they bore me. My life as a baby and a young child was scary because of all the demonic activity happening in the houses where I lived. This was a regular occurrence throughout my life until I engaged with Ian Clayton and learned from him. It was at that point that I was able to back off from the demonic realm and not look at it anymore, and turn my intent towards the realms of the Kingdom and the angelic Realm.

I asked the Father to open my eyes to the realms of the Kingdom, which He did, and it was such a relief to not see into the demonic realm all the time! Then, my husband died, and the next day he was in my kitchen! That was a problem for me as I wasn't allowed to talk to dead people as per my instruction within the religious system. I could see he wasn't dead, he was definitely alive, had a bunch of scrolls in his hand and was instructing me. I heard his conversation with the Father through cardiognosis before he got to me. My husband died at a quarter to twelve at night and at four o'clock the next morning we all went to bed. Yahweh spoke to me, through Wisdom, in my right ear and said I would walk in a double anointing and He said He wanted me to take over this ministry. After He said that I saw what looked like vultures flying in a circle and waiting to grab this ministry.

The next day the apostolic people I was walking with at the time came to visit me and I asked them who was taking over the Church. After some discussion, I told them that I had heard from God and felt I should take it over. I was very single-minded and they hastily agreed with me. Then I spoke about money and asked how much I was going to earn because my husband got the salary. They told me I needn't worry about that but I insisted because I wanted to mourn properly without worrying. They said I could earn my husband's salary. We were then able to move on from there. Yahweh then told me to tell everyone I came into contact with, about the encounter with my husband, the way the walls opened and how he was standing there with the scrolls and what he looked like. I did that and it got me into a lot of trouble!

I found it interesting that it was the ministers and the preachers of the gospel that began to have a problem with what I was saying. They called me a Jezebel, a maverick, a white witch and a cult leader amongst other things. My spiritual mom at the time advised me to write down what I saw in case I forgot it. I've remembered every detail and I can step back into that place where my husband engaged with me because there is no time and space in that realm. I can see, smell and hear everything that happened. It's crystal clear. Nothing is embellished, nothing has changed or moved because it was an encounter. I'm grateful for that encounter because it allowed me to step into a realm that I've always stepped into, but now, through the encounter with my very own husband, I had more understanding.

I've always seen Yeshua and I know what He looks like, which is not at all like the pictures we've seen! To a degree, I've seen Holy Spirit and I've encountered the Father's as I lay at His feet. I've also encountered angels and seen many other things. I've kept quiet about all of this but now we're in a place where we can speak about it and at the same time keep within the boundaries of Scripture and of Holy Spirit. Engaging with Tutors and Governors is all found within the world of Yahweh. It is not our world, it is not the earthly world, it is all sitting within the confines of the world of Yahweh – it is huge! Within His world we have different Tutors and Governors:

The Ancient Ones
The Ever-living Ones
The Men of Old
The Spirits of Just Men Made Righteous
Men in White Linen
The Shin Elohim
The Beni Elohim
Angels

We can engage with these Tutors and Governors and there are many Scriptures which speak about them. They are part of the Cloud of Witnesses and are around us all the time.

In **Galatians 4:1-7** we read, "Now I say that the heir, as long as he is a child, does not differ at all from a slave, though he is master of all, but is under guardians and stewards until the time appointed by the father. Even so we, when we were children, were in bondage under the elements of the world. But when the fullness of the time had come, God sent forth His Son, born of a woman, born under the law, to redeem those who were under the law, that we might receive the adoption as sons."

Hebrews 12:1 says, "Therefore we also, since we are

surrounded by so great a cloud of witnesses, let us lay aside every weight, and the sin which so easily ensnares us, and let us run with endurance the race that is set before us."

Scripture says we're surrounded by a great Cloud of Witnesses, meaning that they are all around us and not just in Heaven; the Kingdom of Heaven is at hand, so when I say they surround us, it's a duality. They are there but they also appear here. That realm comes and the veil between that realm and this realm gets really thin and they appear around us but are still in that realm. Sometimes there are those from the Cloud of Witnesses who walk amongst us. The Men of Old have taken their bodies as well as the Everliving Ones and they have just kept on living, like the Desert Fathers. They have never died and are five or six hundred years old in the natural. Their bodies are starting to metamorphosise into immortality and same desert fathers going see-through, so they hide that with their clothing.

Enoch is one of the men of old because he took his body with him. Both Moses and John the Revelator took their bodies. Every generation on this earth has this happen because there has to be a record of the mysteries, a record of those who have been inserted or have learned how to take their god-bodies up and down.

We've read that Enoch walked with God for 365 years but we need to remember that numbers in the Scriptures mean something. 365 talks about the fullness of time and not necessarily a specific time frame of years. Enoch walked with Yahweh for many years and some Jews say Enoch was in the face of Yahweh for 365 years. The people in those days also lived much longer because there was still a vestige of the glory sitting in the body of Adam and subsequently in all of those who came after him. Their bodies still didn't decay as much as ours do now, because sin wasn't so rampant although it did become corrupt in the days of Noah. There was a closeness between the two realms and their bodies still carried a record of Heaven and so it took 930 or 960 years before their bodies would die. Most of them didn't die because they were sick but because they had finished living, and fulfilled their destiny scrolls.

Who were the Ancient Ones? We know that Melchizedek is an Ancient One and not a Man in White Linen. Ian mentioned that Melchizedek was one of the two covering Cherubs with Lucifer being the other one. Lucifer decided that there was not one thing that he didn't know about God and through his will decided to do what he did. Where does that place the Ancient Ones? Melchizedek, Metatron, and others were in realms that came before the Eternal Realm. Wisdom was with God before any of these ways; before the Eternal Realm, before the beginning of His ways, before the works of old, before the Beginning and before the Everlasting, Wisdom was with Him. Wisdom was a master craftsman and Yahweh's daily delight who delighted in the sons of men. Job was from first creation which is before the seven days of creation.

It is said of Melchizedek that he was without mother or father or beginning of days and he was made unto Yahweh. He was the first one that Yahweh fashioned into the likeness of the full form of His own son, taking on the sonship role, to carry the responsibility of the Treasury Rooms of Heaven. People often think Melchizedek is Yeshua, but he was just in the form of a son to fulfil his responsibility in Heaven, not to come to earth to die.

Yeshua is not one of the Ever-living Ones. He is the Son of the Father and from the Father, together with the Ruach. There are at least 250 other races of Beings in the Council Rooms of Heaven. When Lucifer started to corrupt he was able to influence a few of those races which still give us problems today.

Metatron has been here from the foundation of everything associated with Yahweh's world. Metatron, as an Ancient One, was engaging with everything in these realms. Before there was a world they were there. Metatron sits at the gate of the mountain of the secrets of Yahweh. As the Father would step off His throne He would take off His robes of glory, and those robes of glory created a golden mountain where He embedded the secrets. He took the keys to the secrets and gave them to Metatron and told him to mentor and steward His people until they would be mature enough to walk in the secrets.

Day two of creation wasn't a good day according to the Scriptures, because that was when Lucifer began to fall. Metatron lost two keys because when Lucifer fell he took the keys of death and of hell which is what put us into bondage at the fall. When Yeshua came He went into the grave, His body metamorphosised, He went into the depths of the earth, set the captives free and took back the keys of death, hell and the grave. We would have been in a perpetual state of sin and death, with no opportunity to get saved other than to offer sacrifices once a year to be free. **Genesis 2:4**, when God created *shamayim* and the earth in that day when He made the earth and the heavens, He created man again and in that day, which is day eight, Lucifer fell. The earth, as we know it, was created in day eight and the priests would offer up their sacrifices in the Holiest of Holies by taking take the blood and putting it on the mercy seat for the forgiveness of sin for the Jews for one year. I read in an ancient document that the High Priest would actually *pass through* the veil in the temple and into day two of creation. It would take the Priest most of his adult life to learn how to step through the six-inch veil or curtain.

Metatron was there from the foundation of everything and he stands there as a Tutor and Governor, not as a gatekeeper. The heir is no different from a slave, though he is master of all, he is under Tutors and Governors or Stewards until the time appointed by the Father. That depends on us. Whenever there's a shift in an Age, we will have these Tutors and Governors begin to engage with the face of the earth. We are currently in day eight of creation and on the 22nd of December 2021 we experienced a shift into the Thirteenth Age which is the final Age leading into day nine which we haven't arrived at yet. The shift occurred and the Seraphim were released because every time there is a shift into the next Age, these Tutors and Governors begin to engage with humanity on the face of the earth. They come from the world of Yahweh into our Age and into our day and begin to engage with us. So many people are taking pictures of Seraphim from all over the face of the earth. We are hearing of wars and rumours of wars and there are many things taking place, but it is not the end of the world, it's the end of an Age.

There is going to be an end because we're going to be creating a new Heaven and a new Earth. This is good news, not bad news! We're going to see a lot of engaging being done by these Ancient Ones, the Ever-living Ones, the Men of Old, and Spirits of Just Men Made Righteous. These last two will engage a lot with humanity on the face of the Earth and when they do, they don't have any reference for our sin, they just wait for an engagement. They don't see and they don't care about it, just as the angels don't care if we sin. They have no reference for it so they just wait until we engage with them and then they turn towards us. We might think they are far away but they're not. They're waiting for us to engage with them.

Angels are often seen in our meetings and around us to see what we are doing. This happens when we unpack our mountains which automatically open a door. When we begin to worship we are terraforming in the Realms of the Kingdom and angels come because they love to hear what we're saying. In fact, there are also Scribing Angels that scribe what we're saying. Whenever we have a meeting and talk about the Kingdom Realms there will be a flurry of angels present wanting to hear what we have to say about them. Other times when we're in corporate worship and the Realms open up they come in because we've unpacked a mountain and the door is open. They worship with us and engage with us because they love to worship Yahweh if we worship Yahweh, which is why song choice is so important. It really does matter. When we're singing about ourselves they can't worship with us because they can't worship us! When we start singing to Yahweh and about Him, how He is holy and how Yeshua's blood is powerful and when we honour Him like that in song, the angels automatically engage with us because they love to worship Him.

When I start singing worship songs about when I looked upon the trees and I heard the flutter, I knew You were near or I worship because there was the sound echoing in the mountains. It's good, but worship is about holiness. It's about Him. The minute we put "I" into the equation, the angels can't worship with us. We've got to come into His presence with thanksgiving and into His courts with praise and then into the Holy Place which is the Holiest of Holies. At that place, no sin can go in and no sweat of the body is allowed in that place, because it's a vestige of flesh. No flesh can enter in. It's got to be in a place of holiness and when we step in, into this place of holiness, because of the blood, it's in that place that the angels worship with us in joyful abandon.

We went through a two-year period at The Altar, here in Durban, South Africa, where the angels sang with us in every single meeting. They would also play instruments and it was fantastic. One Sunday they didn't sing with us and I grabbed all of the musicians and asked them what was wrong because there was no angelic presence! I was very determined that worship had to be done correctly. The angels were very playful; they would move around us, touch us, touch with our hair and we also had rain fall in our meetings. Oil, gold and feathers also fell in our meetings and it was crazy. I used to tell the congregation not to speak about what was happening as it was so unusual and it was during this time that I was called a Jezebel cult leader. The veil between this realm and that realm was so thin that we could see those who had gone before us like it is written in **Hebrews 12:1**, and they were part of the Cloud of Witnesses cheering us on.

I don't remember the day it started easing off, but I think it was just that Yahweh gave us great grace in a season and a time where there was a transitioning of pastors and it solidified the church in the glory. Now, we are beginning to see it manifesting now in everyday life as we engage in the Realms of the Kingdom and living an ascended life. During our meetings gold dust and gold bits would fall and I remember picking up an actual gold nugget. It was heavy!

We began pursuing the gold and silver and the feathers and suddenly that grace just lifted. I spoke to a mentor about this and he said that when Melchizedek, together with the angelic who surround him, was trying to engage with the body at that time because he is the keeper of the treasury rooms of heaven, they were trying to engage with the Body of Christ for the transferal of the wealth to come into the Body. We were so busy looking at the signs, we forgot that signs always point us to a destination. We stopped at the sign and didn't look for the destination. Even though we missed the mark, it was an amazing few years. Now, if there is gold and silver in our meetings, I ask Melchizedek what he's wanting to say because we can see a manifestation of his presence!

When there's a shift in an Age, we know that the Heavenly Beings are wanting to engage on the face of the Earth and we need to turn and actively engage with them. We don't summon them into this realm; in other words, we don't summon Metatron and talk to him in the physical world. If we do that then we are no different to Saul who summoned the witch of Endor and told her to call up Samuel into this realm. Our engagement with these Beings, these Governors and Tutors, has to be in that Realm. If we start summoning them in this natural realm then we are dealing with familiar spirits. Who we are then engaging with is not really the Being we called – they are something else. I'm seeing a lot of this at the moment where people have engaged in this natural realm with an angelic being they are called that has walked into the room and these Beings start asking strange questions like, "What if God died on the cross and not Yeshua? What if the blood that was shed was actually God's blood, not Yeshua's blood? What if His name isn't Yahweh? What if Yeshua's name is Yehoshua which means 'God saves'?" I've noticed that there's a strange move at the moment, of removing

Yeshua and His blood. When people call up those Beings to talk to them here the Being sounds right, it looks right, it's shiny and bright but it's moving Yeshua out of the equation and sometimes even moving Holy Spirit out by saying it's *all* about the Seven Spirits. We have to be so careful and walk circumspectly and in holiness.

When I see angels, it's in the Realm of my Father that I'm speaking of because I'm arcing in both realms. However, as soon as I see them, I know that I'm seeing through the veil of His flesh. The two realms are joined together because of that veil and I'm engaging in that Realm while I'm here on earth. If I were to call my husband to come and see me, that would be necromancy. I might call up a familiar which would put me in a lot of trouble. I have never called my husband but he sometimes would appear and every time he did, he would instruct me. Once he asked me why I had done something in a particular way and I replied that I had to do it in that fashion because I had no one to help me. He turned and behind him I saw many people, the Cloud of Witnesses and angelic Beings. He said, "They are all here to help you". I never called him. He came and spoke to me. In the fifteen years that he's transitioned I've spoken to him maybe five times and each time I saw him he instructed me as a Man in White Linen. He's instructed me as one who has gone before me, but he's never spoken to me like a husband. I then understood the Scripture where it says there is no giving and taking of marriage in heaven. I could marry ten husbands and there would be no issue in heaven because it's not about husbands. I'm connected to him because we have a connection in the Spirit but it isn't a romantic connection, it's a pure love connection and a heart to heart connection. He speaks to me as someone who instructs. If he spoke to me in any other way, I would rebuke it and tell it to get out.

If we engage with the angelic while in the realm of this world and under the sun and we call them to us to do our bidding, it will most likely be a familiar spirit because of the corruption in this realm. We will be channelling a familiar spirit which is why Scripture in the Old Testament was clear. We must not do this. The witch of Endor did this and the people who call up someone's great-granny do this. They're channelling the familiars that were around great-granny and know everything about her. We must be careful we don't do the same thing.

I see people go online and announce that they'll be going live to tell everyone what Archangel Michael had shared with them. Honestly, if Michael wanted to say something he would tell us all and we would all be shifting and turning towards him. We must be so careful not to build these fanciful fantasy worlds that are not real. We create them through the breath of our mouth. We create worlds that have Pizza Huts and Christmas parks and dinosaur parks because these things are familiar to us and we're comfortable with them so it becomes 'in heaven as it is on earth.' This is a problem because we have taken a lot of our undealt with mindsets and ideas and have labelled them with mystical terminology and thought it was all okay. This is not meant to frighten us. When we engage with something that we are not sure of, we can easily run it past someone whom we trust; not someone who thinks like us and who will agree with us!

My husband used to teach that every river needs river banks because without them the river becomes a marsh and it becomes difficult because not everything can grow in a marsh. Riverbanks are not evil, they are necessary. However, if the riverbanks are so restrictive that the river cannot go where it needs to flow, the river will break the banks and run right through them. The riverbank has to be able to flow with the river while still remaining a riverbank.

We've been flowing along in Christianity, through Pentecostalism which led into the Charismatic movement and suddenly we made a sharp turn into mysticism. Then we encounter the Seraphim and we turn again but we're still within the riverbanks. We are all still learning new terminology and my mentor corrects my verbiage when he needs to. Once I was on an aeroplane and was bored so I stepped off the plane and onto what I called my surfboard. My mentor corrected me and told me it was my dais and was full of diamonds. I was shocked that he knew what I was talking about! We need these people to help us and counsel us with the formation of the emanation of all that we get to do. We must also look in Scripture because it's all there, sitting in mystery. We will then be able to walk circumspectly with what we're doing. It doesn't need to go on social media, because it's the glory of the Father to conceal it and the honour of kings to search out a matter. **Proverbs 25:2**.

When I went to England Yahweh told me that I needed to go into hiddenness and take the then Church underground. I didn't know what that meant and just thought we were going to be persecuted. For those who know me know that I'm not at all keen at being persecuted! At the time I didn't know what hiddenness was all about, but now I do because we teach about the likes of Metatron and Melchizedek who have keys. The Church would just not understand it if they heard about the things we are teaching. The secrets stay secret so I cannot put it out there. If someone were to do a Google search on me there is very little about my teachings because Yahweh told me to go into hiddenness. I only share the things in mystery and the secrets of Yahweh to those who have the same DNA and will run with it and create a New Heaven and a New Earth, together.

My ancestors did strange things. I had a great-uncle who was a white witch and passed his gift on to the rest of the family which resulted in everybody floating out of their bodies and doing crazy things. Whenever someone was going to die, a member of their family would be seen walking along the passage or sitting on the bed. Demons and familiar spirits were rife! However, many of my family members did come to know Christ and died in Christ which means they were part of those who were cheering us on.

The Cloud of Witnesses is not just Abraham, Isaac, Melchizedek, Jacob, etc., it's also our people who were in Christ and have become part of our Cloud of Witnesses which surround us. They still have a mandate with us. When my husband transitioned, I saw him and then my youngest child saw him. One day he said, "Mom, dad came to fetch me last night and showed me some things around the face of the earth." This should be normal.

When my youngest son got married Ian Clayton came to preach and marry him and his wife to be. During the ceremony there was a lightning bolt that struck which I thought was going to do us damage but it was from heaven! It was so loud! It struck the land of the house next door and popped some of the electricity. Ian immediately turned and asked, "Did you see? Did you see?" I saw nothing because I was trying to make sure every guest was still standing. Ian's arm hair were standing on end but as the mother of the bridegroom, I didn't have time to look into the heavenly realms. Ian said that Ron, my husband, had just come on that lightning bolt. The weather forecast had said it would be sunny but meanwhile there were clouds moving rapidly across the sky and big drops of rain fell. They stopped and suddenly the lightning struck over. Ian had never met Ron but knew that Ron had arrived on the lightning bolt to over see his son's marriage. Ron still has a mandate over his child. Ian also said that Ron has a new position in heaven and had been promoted. When he went to heaven he entered into the Chancellor's Court because of what he carried on the earth. He entered into the same Realm of Government in Heaven as he carried on earth. This is why I saw him carrying all the scrolls.

What are the roles of all these Beings that surround us? They watch us and testify in court, they testify in the heavens, they testify around us and they take part in the journey we are on. They rejoice with us and become part of our testators; they testify about what we're doing. Lizzie, my daughter-in-law, has given me permission to share her story. Her mom died suddenly. There was no drama; one minute she was making lunch and the next she stopped living and transitioned. She had come to know Yeshua two years before but it was devastating for Lizzie and her brothers, as well as for us because Jed's dad had been dead for a couple of years and now his wife's mother had died. They struggled greatly over the passing of such a lovely, beautiful, gentle and sweet lady. I was in England at the time and said to Yahweh that Jed and Lizzie were really struggling over her death and that I really needed to see Rose, her mother. I started to engage, but not in this corrupted realm which would have summoned a familiar spirit. I stepped through the veil and said, "Father can I see Rosie." This was the first time in my life I actually asked to see someone. I immediately saw what looked like a huge golden portal that had a railing around it and Rosie was holding on to the railing and looking over into the portal. She looked spectacular. She was so beautiful and shining that for a minute I thought she was the Being of Wisdom until I realised it was Rosie. She was standing there holding on to the golden railing and speaking to Lizzie and Jed saying, "Come on my Lizzie, you can do this. Come on Lizzie and Jed, you can do this." She was cheering them on. I was standing in that realm watching her even though I was still in my room physically. I called out to her and said, "Rosie, you look amazing!" She turned to me, looked at me seriously, which is not in her character to do, and said, "I'm not called that here." I left before asking her what her heavenly name is. I phoned my daughter-in-law and told her I had just seen her mom. I told her that when she went to bed that night she needed to ask Yahweh if she could see her mom in her dream world. She did this and dreamt about her mom. She was a different girl after that encounter. I didn't call Rosie. I engaged with her on that side of the veil, not under the sun.

In **Genesis 18:1** we read, "Then the Lord appeared to him by the terebinth trees of Mamre, as he was sitting in the tent door in the heat of the day." We must remember that the tent door, the house, is the opening into a realm. It's not sitting in the heat of the day in a desert. In **verse 2** we read, "So he lifted his eyes and looked, and behold, three men were standing by him; and when he saw them, he ran from the tent door to meet them, and bowed himself to the ground." In other words, Abraham was in his tent but then he was in the tent door, the *Dalet* of his heavenly tent, his house, his being.   When he saw the three men standing there he ran from the tent door which was from the place of who he is, to meet them. He bowed before them and they came into this realm. In **Genesis 18:3** we read, "And said, 'My Lord, if I have now found favour in Your sight, do not pass on by Your servant."' The name 'Lord' in this Scripture is the same name as the Beni Elohim which means Sons of Elohim. **Verse 4** says, "Please let a little water be brought, and wash your feet, and rest yourselves under the tree." The tree is a whole other subject as well. **Verse 5** reads, "And I will bring a morsel of bread, that you may refresh your hearts. After that, you may pass by, in as much as you have come to your servant." They said, "Do as you have said." Abraham hurried into the tent to Sarah and again, this is a transition from that realm to this realm. He saw them in that realm and then they manifested physically. **Genesis 18:6-8** says, "So Abraham hurried into the tent to Sarah and said, "Quickly, make ready three measures of fine meal; knead it and make cakes." And Abraham ran to the herd, took a tender and good calf, gave it to a young man, and he hastened to prepare it. So he took butter and milk and the calf which he had prepared, and set it before them; and he stood by them under the tree as they ate."

It has been said that the bread Abraham had made was like the shew bread that was in the Tabernacle. Scripture tells us that they ate. Angels generally do not eat because they don't need to eat to live. The Men in White Linen will eat; not because they need to live but because of their function here and now in the other realm. The Bible tells us that we must be careful how we engage with strangers and people we don't know because we might be entertaining angels unaware.

In **Genesis 19:1** we read, "Now the two angels came to Sodom in the evening, and Lot was sitting in the gate of Sodom. When Lot saw them, he rose to meet them, and he bowed himself with his face toward the ground." Again, when we look at Lot sitting in the gate, he's not necessarily just in the gate or doorway of that city. The people of Sodom had opened a gate into sexual corruption and it was almost as if

Lot was sitting at that gate, being a gatekeeper. In **verse 2-3** we read, "And he said, 'Here now, my lords, please turn in to your servant's house and spend the night, and wash your feet; then you may rise early and go on your way.' But he insisted strongly; so they turned in to him and entered his house. Then he made them a feast, and baked unleavened bread, and they ate." The term 'my lords' refers again to Beni Elohim. Because the men of the city had opened the gate into sexual corruption and immorality they immediately wanted to engage with the Beings because of the corrupt seed-line of male on male sexual activity. This activity brings about a trading into the stars which gives them power.

In **Ezekiel 10:2** we read about two men in white linen. In **Daniel 12:5** Daniel saw two men. In **Matthew 17:2-4** we read, "And He was transfigured before them. His face shone like the sun, and His clothes became as white as the light. And behold, Moses and Elijah appeared to them, talking with Him. Then Peter answered and said to Jesus, 'Lord, it is good for us to be here; if You wish, let us make here three tabernacles: one for You, one for Moses, and one for Elijah.'" Some translations say that His face shone 'other' when He transfigured and His clothes shone. When I saw my husband, that's what he looked like. His clothes were shining and lightning bolts were shooting out. That's the garment of righteousness which looks like a robe. Both Moses and Elijah took their bodies with them which makes them part of the Ever-Living Ones or the Men of Old.

It is good to work in honour with these Beings. When Ian Clayton first met Abraham he addressed him incorrectly and Abraham corrected him. The same thing happened to me when I met Melchizedek while I was dealing with some financial things. I told people that he was very grumpy, meaning it as a joke. Two years later I saw him again regarding the same issue. He just looked at me and told me that I had misrepresented him. I apologised profusely and asked him to forgive me. He's not a little guy, he's this huge presence and very serious and austere. When I spoke to Ian about what had happened Ian said he had never seen Melchizedek in any position other than one who is austere and serious about the Treasury rooms of Heaven. He's not a killjoy, he's just an austere being. We must be careful not to walk in dishonour by giving them a nickname because there is something so very powerful about a name. Our name gives us the character of what and who we are, through breath. We then shorten our name which just doesn't work. Sometimes people meet angels and give them silly names. These are angelic beings and need to be treated accordingly.

In **Luke 9:32-36** we read, "But Peter and those with him were heavy with sleep; and when they were fully awake, they saw His glory and the two men who stood with Him. Then it happened, as they were parting from Him, that Peter said to Jesus, 'Master, it is good for us to be here; and let us make three tabernacles: one for You, one for Moses, and one for Elijah'—not knowing what he said. While he was saying this, a cloud came and overshadowed them; and they were fearful as they entered the cloud. And a voice came out of the cloud, saying, 'This is My beloved Son. Hear Him!' When the voice had ceased, Jesus was found alone. But they kept quiet, and told no one in those days any of the things they had seen."

There are so many passages in the Scriptures that mention the Cloud of Witnesses who partake in what is going on as Tutors and Mentors. When Yeshua died on the cross all the graves opened and the Men in White Linen came out to walk among the people. The Jewish texts say that they walked amongst the people for nearly two weeks. Some of the Cloud of Witnesses were walking amongst them teaching, governing and preparing. Why were they there? Because there was a new Age. Yeshua had died, the veil had been torn and there was a new Age ushered in with the angelic visible all around.

In **Mark 16:4-8** it says, "But when they looked up, they saw that the stone had been rolled away—for it was very large. Entering the tomb, they saw a young man clothed in a long white robe sitting on the right side; and they were alarmed.

But he said to them, 'Do not be alarmed. You seek Jesus of Nazareth, who was crucified. He is risen! He is not here. See the place where they laid Him. But go, tell His disciples—and Peter—that He is going before you into Galilee; there you will see Him, as He said to you.' So they went out quickly and fled from the tomb, for they trembled and were amazed. And they said nothing to anyone, for they were afraid."

The young man could have been an angel but he could also have been one of the men that have gone before, one of the Ancient Ones. This was a transitional time; something had moved and changed. Some people have asked about the Magi – who were they? Where did they come from? Magi are often called the God-men. When we look to see where they fit in, we see them in a realm between the Eternal Realm and the Beginning of His Way. There were twelve of them. Three stayed behind while nine came through following the star. The three that stayed behind are the king of Peace, the king of Righteousness, and the king of Salem. The king of Salem is Melchizedek. The nine that came through all of the realms came through the East Gate. They came into creation and into our day when Yeshua was born.

We now have three of the Magi walking on the face of the earth. I saw them a few years ago during a meeting. I saw three of them looking down through a portal. I told Ian what I had seen and he said the three Magi were in our meeting. They had been walking on the face of the earth waiting for the new Age and to see a people through whom Yahweh can begin to land something on the face of the earth again, people who are ready for what's about to come and who know how to rise up as kings and as lords, who are going to govern in the Realms of the Kingdom.

Chapter 7
Signs, Seasons, Days And Years

Ephesians 1:7-10 says, "In Him we have redemption through His blood, the forgiveness of sins, according to the riches of His grace which He made to abound toward us in all wisdom and prudence, having made known to us the mystery of His will, according to His good pleasure which He purposed in Himself, that in the dispensation of the fullness of the times He might gather together in one all things in Christ, both which are in heaven and which are on earth—in Him."

I love how Scripture says "in the dispensation of the fullness of times." To get an idea of what times we're talking about we must have a look at when it was first mentioned. In **Genesis 1** we read about what happened in the beginning and it's the remembrance of who we were before we were here. **Genesis 1:14** says, "Then God said, 'Let there be lights in the firmament of the heavens to divide the day from the night; and let them be for signs and seasons, and for days and years.'" The word 'lights' should really read luminaries or illuminations. If we look at the interlinear meanings on the Blue Letter Bible App and look at the ancient texts we see that it is not the sun, moon and stars. It is lights. It is us. Luminaries. **Jeremiah 1:5**, I knew you before you were in your mother's womb. We were the ones with a god-body who shone in this manifested state of glory within Yahweh. Where we read, "Let there be lights in the firmament of the heavens to divide the day from the night," this doesn't mean dividing the sunshine from the darkness. I'd like to suggest that the division of day and night is the division of night when we engage in the *choshek* and the day which holds the secrets of the Lord. This is a time of engaging with the mysteries of Yahweh so when we wake up in the day, we can walk it out and the secrets of Yahweh begin to be manifested as an emanation through us.

So, the Scripture says let the luminaries, which is you and I in our first estate, be in the firmament of heaven to divide the day and the night. The 'lights' didn't divide the day and night or light and darkness because in **Genesis 1:16** we read that God made two great lights; the greater light and the lesser light to rule the night and the day. In **verse 14** we are reading about something totally different – the luminaries are to divide the secrets and the mysteries. **Genesis 1:14** also says, "Let them be for signs and seasons, and for days and years." What does this Scripture speak of?

There are four chambers of the luminaries -
Signs
Seasons
Days
Years

These four chambers can only be accessed through relationship with Yahweh and as a luminary we are to be a sign, a season, a day and a year.

Light in Hebrew is *ma'or* מאור which means a luminary or an illuminous body.
Firmament in Hebrew is *raqia* רְקִיעַ which is the expanse or the vault of heaven supporting the waters above. We can re-read the text in this way: Let the illuminous body be in the expanse of the vaults of heaven which support the waters above.

Signs in Hebrew is *oth* אות - a distinguishing mark, a banner, a miracle or in a sense something appearing.
Season in Hebrew is *mo'ed* מועד - an anointed or sacred season or place.
Days in Hebrew is *yom* יוֹם - yesterday, today, tomorrow, perpetually present.
Years in Hebrew is *sana* שנים - a division of time, a measure of time, a revelation of time.

Signs are interesting. We become a display of the goodness and the glory of God within creation to display all that we are and who we are in His Kingdom. We become a sign. How do we do this?

SIGNS

If we walk in our celestial body, terrestrial body, natural and carnal body, and spiritual body, they all culminate in our god-body and we begin to operate in this body within our cube. Our natural body is able to travel across the world by itself without needing the silver cord. It uses the golden bowl. The silver cord gets broken when you get born from above. Our various bodies engage with one another where we also have an up and down connection between our god-body and our carnal body. The down part is our carnal body sitting on the face of the earth and the 'up' part is our god-body which reaches into who we are. If we all operated in the North, South, East, West and the up and down, backwards and forwards, then these Rings of Power would all be twirling around us in circles like a wheel within a wheel. If we walk in this fashion, it becomes a sign which is a distinguishing mark, a banner or a sense of appearing. We, as firmaments, are supposed to be a sign into creation.

We are kings and priests, legislators and oracles. In 'old-speak' an oracle was called an intercessor. In 'new-speak' we are oracles because we reach into the future. As we engage with our carnal and physical body together with who we are as kings, priests, legislators and oracles we come into full sonship. These distinguishing signs oscillate and move around us, up and down and distinguish us from everything that is around us. This is what the luminaries were called to be - a distinguishing sign or a sense of appearing. Scripture says let THEM be for SIGNS. We become a display of the goodness and the glory of Yahweh within creation. Where is creation in all of this? It's sitting under our feet and we display who we are, what we are and whose we are in His Kingdom. We become a sign and a wonder.

SEASONS

I've heard one of my mentors speak about this subject and as I've been mulling over it and engaging with it I've suddenly understood it and have been able to operate in it, because it's become part of who I am and I can then teach it. I never teach about something I don't know. Our seasons are made up of spring, summer, autumn/fall and winter. I have heard people say they are in the winter of their life or marriage, or they're in a spring or summer season in their circumstances, but we are not subject to the sun so when we speak like that we begin to bring ourselves under the sun. Seasons are subject to us because we are the administrators of a kingdom within each season.

As I write this, in the southern hemisphere, we are walking into the season of autumn. This season in the natural, under the sun, will start becoming colder and the leaves will start to fall. We are administrators of the kingdom that sits within this season, to shift the season and to shift what is going on within the season. In other words, even though we're going into a natural season of autumn, as luminaries and as those who walk into their god-body as a sign and a distinguishing thing, we are now going to sit in the government of administration within the kingdom within autumn, that season of autumn, and we're going to learn how to shift the seasons. With each season comes different things; governmentally and under the sun things happen but we can stand within each season and govern.

As a physical being we stand within time but as a spirit being we engage and move the seasons around us outside of time. We stand in the realm of autumn but we start to govern in the realms of the kingdom and we govern the kingdom realm of autumn. I found it so interesting to see that seasons are subject to me.

When we look at the seasons we see that a ladder of time runs through them. If we're under the sun, then time will affect us. If we're above the sun, the ladder of time doesn't affect us because time is a Being whom we can engage with. The numbers 1-12 on a clock are each represented by an angel which governs that particular time. We've heard of 'father time' but now we know that time is an actual Being. We can engage with time by sitting in autumn and reaching into time and telling it we are not governed by time but that we govern it. As we sit and engage with the Being of time we are sitting both in time and in autumn knowing we are not subjected to what it looks like and what it's going to be like.

My son said to me the other day that he had heard me talking about governing time and felt that February had been a very long month. Traditionally February is a short month but I had begun to govern the days and said to time that it had to listen to me as I had many things to do so he had done the same. I didn't want to rush ahead and wonder where the year had gone. I asked my son if we were still in March and I couldn't believe we still had over a week to go before April! There had been so much going on and I felt like I had accomplished a kingdom-load of stuff and I still had another week and a half to do it! What a joy! Time doesn't drag or speed up because there are things to do, places to go and people see. I'm learning how to sit as a luminary, as a sign and as a season.

Our summer has been spectacular and we've had the best rains. We've governed the summer so well here that the proper rains have come like they used to years ago. In autumn we're going to see the same thing and we're going to see a proper winter with good snow or cold weather which gets rid of germs and then we can step into spring. As I look at the ladder of time I look into autumn and tell myself I'm going to sit in the government of autumn and say, "Autumn, I love you and I honour you." I sit in the gate of autumn which brings in the cold and the shift in season because we need it but I'm also going to tell it that as I sit in the physical realm, in the gate of autumn, I'm talking as a distinguishing sign saying, "No more are we going to have any more pandemics. It must end."

How do we do this? How do we, as manifesting, emanating sons, sit in this place of governing the season of autumn? The northern hemisphere will be entering spring which can bring allergies. We must govern the kingdom that sits around spring, above the sun, as a son, as a king, as a lord, as a priest, as a legislator and an oracle and as a sign. We must sit in spring and say, "I'm going to govern both my body and creation around me and it's going to be a glorious spring and a glorious summer." As we learn how to govern we're not only changing things so that we don't have a damaging winter or summer but we're learning how to govern in the place where we bring the earth back into balance. As we sit on the face of the earth we're dealing into each kingdom of each season, learning how to govern as luminaries, and as we do that they begin to turn around us in an oscillating circle. In our physical bodies we then stand on the earth learning how to govern the weather and what's going on around us.

Scripture says, "Let them be there to divide the day and the night and for signs and for seasons." We're supposed to be above the sun dealing into things. If we look at the book of Enoch and other ancient books, we read that every season has a gate. The winds have a door which we can walk through. I recently stood in the door of the wind. It was a north/westerly wind and I stood in the gate of that door and told it that I needed it to not blow until a certain time. I knew we needed the wind to bring the rain but I had organized an event and we really couldn't have the windy day that had been forecast. I wasn't manipulating it instead I was sitting as a son telling the wind it could blow everywhere else but wait until the appointed time to blow over our area so it could bring the rain. That's exactly what happened. At the correct time the winds came and by then we had finished with the blow-up jumping castle for the event. The wind listened and waited at the door until the appointed time and then began to fulfil its function. What had happened? I was a luminary, as a sign operating as a legislator, king and priest. I had gone into the gate of the summer wind and had told it to wait. While I was governing I also told it to not do any damage or harm anybody.

DAYS

One day in the house of the Lord is as a thousand days elsewhere – we all know that Scripture. We also know that we are in the eighth moving into the ninth day of creation and we positioned ourselves in each day of creation as we came through each day as luminaries with signs, seasons, days and years upon us through all of those different realms. Why did we do that? It's because we need to know our way back to the beginning of creation, the beginning of His ways, the everlasting etcetera, until we get to creation and into day one, day two and all the way through to day eight. The High priests of the Old Testament would go into the second day of creation when they went through the veil. We're in the eighth day of creation to see the revelation of that day unfolding. Every time we see the words 'that day', it is a new era or a new time or a new 'day'. So, when we see *that day* unfold around us, it's because it is a new season, a new time and a new era that is upon us. We're on the brink of seeing the ninth day of creation. We're sitting in a new day, the 13th Age, but we're heading into the ninth day of creation, a new Heaven and a new Earth. There were millions of years in between all of these 'days', not just one day.

The high priest would position himself in the second day of creation even though he was here in the eighth day. And so really speaking what happens is that we have this synergy happening where we are engaging in all these days, having come as a luminary into this day. On the face of the earth they went through the veil in the tabernacle which represented the veil of His flesh and they would step into the second day of creation. Many of us thought that the priest would step through the veil of the tabernacle and into the holiest of holies, place the blood on the mercy seat and then come back out again. The reason the high priest went through to the second day of creation is because they were positioning themselves in *that day* before corruption happened. Lucifer then brought corruption into day two, but this is where the corruption of Lucifer started.

This is why the high priest would go through the veil because he was literally engaging in how creation should look, engaging in a place of no corruption before Lucifer began to corrupt, to position himself there to help administrate it into the eighth day. In Judaism, this is called *tikkun olam*, תִּיקוּן עוֹלָם which means 'repairers of the world'. This phrase is found in the Mishnah, a body of classical rabbinic teachings compiled in the 3rd Century. The priest would take the non-corrupted day two of creation, the pureness of what it was, and then position himself to bring it back into day eight.

This is why we position ourselves so that when we step back through the veil we are bringing what was there, in that place in the second day of creation, and releasing it into day eight. We must understand the place of the second day of creation, that we're a sign and a season in a day and a year and that we've come to bring something on the face of the earth in the days that we are engaged with as a luminary, delivering it into day eight. We cannot stay in corruption and in the fall and feel sorry for ourselves saying we are all just sinners saved by grace, from the guttermost to the uttermost. This comes from Pentecostalism. We are better than that. We are more than that and the beautiful thing about being in *the Day* is that we can go up and down which is what we're supposed to be doing as luminaries. It's what we're called to do. *A day* means being perpetually present, being in day two and bringing it into day eight and pushing into day nine.

YEARS

Coming into day nine brings us to the place of years. Not into our present calendar year because we're not stuck here. Years is a division of time and a measure of time or a revelation of time. As luminaries, we're in a place where we become a revelation of time to the world around us. There's no time in years because this is above the sun and is a revelation of time – the time that sits outside of time. Time that governs, it's a time to do this, it's a time to do that, it's a time to rejoice, it's a time to be sad, etc. Scripture says that there is nothing new under the sun which is why we have to go above it, for the secrets of Yahweh sit above the sun.

Living outside of the 365 days which make up one year is living in the revelation of time. Living in the future while in my present is living in a revelation of time because time doesn't govern me and I'm living my future right now. When we speak in tongues, read His Word, breathing with the Living Letters and being wrapped around and encompassed by the blood of the Lamb it all helps us to walk out our year according to the perfect will of Yahweh and according to our destiny scroll. We govern our year from the future, from the *olam*. Praying in the Spirit mobilizes our body into light and our Light Being reaches out from within the cube. From the corners of our cube we extend our tent pegs, and we reach out into the *olam*, reaching into the future, taking that scroll and our future and bringing it back into our present. We live from the future in our present.

We are in the centre of our cube, our life, walking out our destiny scroll of our future in our present, walking it out as those who are a sign or a distinguishing mark, a season governing each of these areas through the gate and the door, a day walking into day two to bring perfection back into where we are now and then as one who is not subject to time under the sun, but walking in a revelation of time, reaching into *olam* bringing our future into our present and walking out our destiny. Even if we don't see it fully manifested we're already laying the foundation of what our future looks like for us and our generations to come because we're walking out our future and setting a platform for success. All those who walk with us have no choice but to succeed! We can govern any year from our future and praying in the Spirit is what mobilizes us.

We govern from the cube within us and we're fitly joined together as stones, on which our foundation, the chief cornerstone, is Yeshua. We can also arc from our past into our future. The past is not necessarily all an evil situation, so we can also take our current past, arcing together between them through the door of our present reality on the face of the earth.

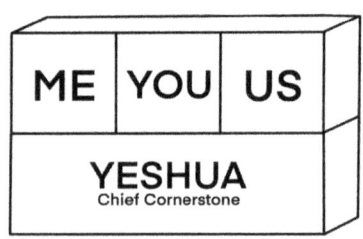

We must deal into our DNA and all the things within us that need to be dealt with, arcing into our future and looking into our destiny scroll, coming through the door of who we are and dealing into our past years so we can live out our future, in our present reality. These are the years that we govern; we don't govern years as in 'time'. Every time Scripture makes reference to numbers it's not speaking about actual numbers.

When we take the number 365, we can add them all up: 3 + 6 + 5 = 14, 1 + 4 = 5. This corresponds to the fifth Hebrew letter *Hey* which means to behold the breath which is represented by a man holding up his arms. Enoch walked with Yahweh for a period of time (365 years) asking Yahweh to reveal Himself through breath so that he could behold His face. Scripture is always written in secret and in mystery. Enoch learned how to govern years and seasons. He was a sign and he knew how to deal into the days. Enoch jumped from day eight, all the way into day two and day one and in fact he went back to the Eternal Place where he saw everything starting from the Beginning. The Hebrews say that Enoch was in the face of God for 365 years.

Job was present before day one and he saw how God made everything because in **Job 38** we read about the morning star first coming out and how Pleiades came out to play. He speaks about the big bear and the little bear which we know today as ursa major and ursa minor. God asked where Job was (**Job 3**) and then said, "You were there," (**Job 1**). In the original Hebrew text, we read that Job was a co-creator with Yahweh.

We were luminaries who were sent into the firmament, the expanse of heaven, supporting the waters above, to divide the day and the night - the secrets and the mysteries of Yahweh - to be a sign, to be a season - governing in the season, to be days and to be years. We are called to be these things, not to look at them and not to be governed by them. In the Church Age, we learned how to be governed by them. All four of these – signs, seasons, days, years – happen through relationship with Yahweh, in relationship with each other and in relationship with all of the saints, all of the angels, all of the Men in White Linen as well as the Beings that show us the Twelve Strands. We are remembering who we are as luminaries. Through relationship we're looking at ourselves as signs, seasons, days and years because we've already divided the day and the night – the mysteries and secrets of Yahweh.

In **Genesis 1:14-15** we read, "Then God said, 'Let there be lights in the firmament of the heavens to divide the day from the night; and let them be for signs and seasons, and for days and years; and let them be for lights in the firmament of the heavens to give light on the earth'; and it was so." This is so we can learn how to govern ourselves as a distinguishing sign, to look into the seasons of the natural and the spiritual and govern the kingdom of each season through this ladder of time, beginning to govern above the sun. This is in the natural and in the spiritual. We can then walk in *the day* – Which day are we stuck in? The days of corruption or the day of perfection and the days of beginning and the days that came before? If we are in those days, we can bring them into day eight so that we can begin to walk into day nine, a new heaven and a new earth.

In years there is no time; it's a revelation of time. The whole issue with years is the division or the measure of time within us, not the months of the year or the years themselves. It's the revelation of what we are walking in now. The revelation for me of time right now, as a governing son is that I'm sitting in this decade saying it's a season of rest. In my season of rest, I'm learning how to rest in chaos. I'm learning how to step into the door of full supply, sitting and drinking and eating from the widow's oil that will begin to feed my generations to come, the sons, the *ben*, (*Beit* and *Nun*) which means the house of the seed. I learned to live in the house of the seed, a generational house because I've learned to separate day and night, mysteries and secrets of Yahweh. I've learned how to be a distinguishing sign. I'm learning how to look like a mature son and how to walk into these days and look at what perfection looks like – not speaking from myself but from the realms of the kingdom.

The seasons are a new one that I'm learning how to govern into. What does it look like, with my body, to sit in the government, in the kingdom of the season of autumn or fall in the southern hemisphere? What does the door into autumn look like? What is its function? What is it supposed to do? What does it look like above the sun? In terms of days, I'm practicing how to arc with the second day of creation you know that I'll be able to walk through walls one of these days. Regarding the years, I do this a lot. The revelation of time, my future, reaching into the *olam* because of the cube. I've gone into the future and taken my past to fix some things in the ladder of my DNA strand of who I am, fixing some hereditary things from the 13th, 15th, 17th and 18th centuries so that I can arc into the future of my generations, bringing it through the door. When I've arced through the door of this reality and into my present on the face of the earth, I can begin to bring it into a new heaven and a new earth.

All of this is to bring us to this place of saying that better is one day in the courts of Yahweh, than a thousand days anywhere else. **Psalm 84:10**, "For a day in Your courts is better than a thousand. I would rather be a doorkeeper in the house of my God than dwell in the tents of wickedness." One day, outside of time, is all of the things that we have discussed. We need to remember the breath of our mouth and say the right things. We must engage with it properly, so that we can step into the fullness of who we were as a luminary to divide the signs, the seasons, the days, the years, so that we can be a sign and a wonder on the face of the earth and so that creation can turn and look at us, and respond eagerly as we are revealed in our maturity.

Chapter 8
Truth About Mammon

Yahweh, within our co-labouring relationship, wanted me to write on this topic of Mammon which is quite timely because of what is unfolding for sons across the nations of the earth. There are two key Pillars within my pursuit as a son that I must mention before I recount the encounter that I had with Mammon. These Pillars were an important part of that engagement which enabled me to behold. These two Pillars are Hunger and Desire and are living Pillars that engage with us. When we arc with these Pillars we can turn to each of them and engage with Hunger and Desire and they arc together within our lives that we may begin to behold and engage the Realms of Yahweh and His Kingdom, which is established within us, so we can release it into creation.

Without Hunger and Desire, we will not, as sons, yearn for the things of the Kingdom. This Hunger and Desire is different from the yearning that we've seen demonstrated within the system of religion, where that yearning is about us wanting to be filled or our desires to be met in our time of need and wanting to feel God's presence here on earth. The Hunger and Desire that I'm speaking about is what David said when he wrote in **Psalm 42:1**, "As the deer pants for the water brooks, so pants my soul for You, O God." That type of Desire is understanding that there is a realm that we can step into in order for us to engage in the fullness of who we are there, and to be seated upon our government to begin to establish encounters that we have here within creation.

Hunger and Desire open up perception which gives us the ability to see, hear and become aware of what Yahweh is doing in us and through us as sons because of our position there. Hunger and Desire begin to channel our pursuit so we can begin to behold encounters. What we know now, through knowledge, without an encounter, could keep us from what we need to know, if we become an expert in our knowledge! If we behold something through knowledge but haven't engaged with the two Pillars of Hunger and Desire, we become satisfied in our understanding and shut ourselves off from the mystery and supply of the Kingdom of Yahweh. We no longer desire the Realms of the Kingdom because we have become satisfied as an expert on that topic and we don't yearn for the greater measure in the realms of truth that are waiting for us to behold. It is imperative for us to continuously engage with Hunger and Desire because they arc together to have a massive impact within our lives.

In **Matthew 5:6** we read, "Blessed are those who hunger and thirst for righteousness, for they shall be filled." Righteousness is one of the Twelve Strands that begins to arc with us within that Being and allows us to engage and to be entangled with it so that we can go up and down within a lifestyle of pursuit and engagement. As in a mirror we behold through the gateways and doorways of each Being and then reflect the Lord's glory as we are being transformed into His image.

In **Psalm 34:8** we read, "Oh, taste and see that the Lord is good; blessed is the man who trusts in Him!" David is talking about an encounter that allows us to see the evidence within us so that we can behold the fruit within creation and become the testimony of what we have engaged with in the Kingdom Realms. We will behold what we encounter. Everything within our pursuit is an encounter that will transform us – not just the knowledge. Knowledge is good but without an encounter, knowledge does not carry the transformation that we, as sons, need to behold within our lives.

I have a relationship with Hunger and Desire who arc with me as I engage with them. They want to engage with us because of the record that we carry. They behold us in our first estate from before the foundation of the earth when we came into creation saying, "Yes," to that burning scroll. The Pillar of Desire gives us supernatural ability to pursue realms hidden in mystery that require faith to explore. Faith was one of the first Beings who presented himself to me and led me on a journey to discover who he is and the mandate that he carries for humanity. He creates a pathway for us into the Realms of the Kingdom and as we grow in maturity we will no longer need the measure of Faith we once had because of our honour in walking with him. I'm not dishonouring Faith; Faith creates pathways to the realms, through engagement, so that by Faith, that pathway becomes part of who we are and we no longer require the measure of Faith we once had to get us there because we understand that the pathway has become part of us. The pathway is also one of the Twelve Strands – The Way – and Faith points us to that because Faith becomes the substance of things hoped for, it becomes the evidence of things not yet seen. Faith is urging us to know and understand who we are so that we can go to the realms and live from that place.

It's been a wonderful journey for me getting to know Faith but in the beginning, I was so intimidated because Faith's opening statement to me was, "I was salvation before Yeshua came." By Faith, before Yeshua came, those who believed would go into a place called Sheol where Abraham's bosom was found. This place was positioned in Faith who held it together until Yeshua came. When Yeshua ascended, I saw through an encounter how Faith opened himself and all who had believed in Faith, before Yeshua, transitioned into Yeshua and they all ascended. Now Faith is charging us to know who we are. Faith arcs together with these Pillars of Hunger and Desire.

During my own journey of engaging with these two Pillars, there was a part of my life I was walking out in this union but at the same time there were so many other things happening spiritually in my life because I want to continuously mature into who I am. This is the place where Yahweh began to behold me before the foundation of the earth when He spoke those words recorded in **Genesis 1**. As I was engaging and working on my DNA I got to the year 1853 and at that place I saw that a trade had taken place upon my family line which removed wealth and riches for something particular and during that trade the spirit of poverty came into my family line. Yahweh showed me that incident as I walked upon my family's generational line and then told me to take responsibility for that trade.

I thought to myself, "Not a chance! I'm not taking responsibility for the choices and decisions that were made. I didn't do it!" The Church does that – we hate taking responsibility and constantly complain that it wasn't us, it was them. They did it. Yahweh just looked at me and said, "Alright, then it's going to have to echo into another generation because the accuser still has the record of that trade which you haven't dealt with, until a son takes on the responsibility and ownership of that trade in order to deal with it and judge it." I accepted that responsibility, took the trade within me, came upon my family line up to the present time and went into the Mobile Court where I took that trade and gave it to Yahweh. I traded that trade for the divorce papers which also symbolises the breath that He breathes in me. When I breathed Him in, the record of that trade was null and void which silenced the accuser. The accuser can no longer accuse me and my family line because of that trade because I said I would take responsibility for it.

Yahweh began to show me that the spirit of poverty has a mandate. Its function is not to kill us. It will keep our head just above water so we can be carriers of that spirit to the next generation. I have an incredible family who will do anything for another family member but I've seen the spirit of poverty being passed on through the generations. Someone had to take responsibility for the trade that took place in 1853, take it upon themselves to go to the Mobile Court and to deal with it in order to receive the papers that silenced the accuser. When I did that there is no more accusation against me and my generation to come.

Receiving the papers for that trade opened the door to an encounter. I was sitting in my office engaging, not having my heart set on anything in particular, just breathing the breath of Yahweh face to face when all of a sudden a door opened. I was invited to step into an arena which I had never seen before. During this encounter, and others that I've had, I wasn't able to say whether I went there physically or if it was in an encounter or a vision because I could feel and behold things around me exactly like I would have in my physical body. In **2 Corinthians 12:2** Paul wrote of himself and said, "I know a man in Christ who fourteen years ago—whether in the body I do not know, or whether out of the body I do not know, God knows—such a one was caught up to the third heaven." During his encounter Paul wasn't sure if he went there physically or not.

While I was in the encounter there was so much space and silence. I saw a whirlwind begin to fashion and form itself – it was both on the inside of me and on the outside where I could see it. The whirlwind began to vibrate under this frequency and I saw that there was substance and matter within the arena I found myself in. I thought to myself that this could be the place where everything that was created, under the sun and above the sun, could have come from. This was substance and matter waiting to arc with created light. While I was there I saw colours and frequencies swirling around me that have no earthly parallel for and a Being emerged and stood in front of me. In this arena, I was standing within my place of government and the Being introduced himself as Mammon and said he wanted to engage with me. I had a bad reaction because of the law of first mention and what I had learned in the Church Age, through a religious system, that Mammon was evil. I had been taught to either choose Mammon or God.

The religious system within the Church Age has misinterpreted the passage of Scripture found in **Matthew 6** concerning Mammon. Prior to **verse 24**, Matthew speaks about prayer and fasting and in **verse 19** mentions the treasures in heaven, or the Treasury Room. In **Matthew 6:24** we read, "No one can serve two masters; for either he will hate the one and love the other, or else he will be loyal to the one and despise the other. You cannot serve God and mammon." The Church decided that God is righteous so Mammon is unrighteous; it has to be done away with because Mammon is a demonic spirit. In this way our belief system has been framed that Mammon is evil.

During my encounter, I was aware of engaging within the union of the Twelve Strands through my relationship with them. These twelve Beings were all present, watching me in this encounter; they were so excited about my opportunity to engage with Mammon! By knowing that the Twelve Strands were there with me I began to step in and my heart opened up to engage in conversation with Mammon. He said to me, "We (plural) have come to serve you. We have been watching your life for the last five years. We have held the record and have watched every trade you have made. We've watched how you've administrated finances going out and coming in and your heart towards certain things. We are now here to serve you." Five years prior to this encounter with Mammon I had dealt with the trade that took place in my family line in 1853! It was then that I had dealt with the spirit of poverty and received my papers so that the accuser no longer had anything to accuse me of, which then led me into my encounter with Mammon. He then said the following, "We can serve you to the measure that you have stewarded us."

A door opened which led me into this journey of discovering a relationship with Mammon who sits within the Realms of Yahweh's Kingdom, administrating wealth and riches in the Treasury that are set up for my family and my family line. Mammon is now engaging me because of how I've been stewarding things over the last five years. This encounter opened a relationship that led me on a journey to behold a realm that was not an option for me until I had dealt with the trade on my family line which kept us in poverty, passing that spirit on to the next generations. When we walk upon creation our mandate is to release and reveal the full nature of Yahweh. By decisions and choices, we begin to receive the inheritance of that portion to establish a kingdom in creation of that which is righteous, of what has wealth and riches and is connected to the Treasury Room of Yahweh that flows in us and through us so we can be that echo-chamber, allowing creation to begin to receive what we are walking out.

It's just not good enough to talk without displaying the result and the fruit. The world is so sick and tired of hearing people say what should be done but they themselves don't display the results of what they are saying should be done.

If something happened to someone in the Church Age, we would take them by the hand and walk with them and trust with them. Now, we trade. We put value on what is impacting us from someone else's life. When we arc together with that person and trade and put value on finances - which is so important to humanity - our trading shifts something in the atmosphere. Mammon watches us and how we steward things. Through this encounter, administrating some things, I've got a new perspective on money. We are positioned above the sun and it wants to behold the light that Yahweh spoke into being. As the sun looks to us and arcs with us we release and display and emanate that light. The sun takes that light and emanates it into creation, changing the frequency of chaos, to bring it into the glorious freedom and liberty. In the same way, we are seated within the realm of our government when it comes to money, which is under the sun and in corruption. I now have a new perspective on money and I see money wanting to serve me because of my position in the Kingdom Realms, arcing with Mammon. Trading is now a joy.

I was chatting to some people about trading and they were saying that they had a limited budget so if they traded they wouldn't be able to buy food or pay their bond. That is logical and makes sense but we cannot confine our lives to this thing we've created and move around in, because it will control us and we'll never be able to give an amount outside of that budget which means we will probably not be able to give at all. This means that we'll live life according to a system and structure which is positioned and tangled into the earth's system and serve money in its corrupted and fallen state.

Money, in a corrupted and fallen state, is not Mammon. They cannot even be mentioned in the same sentence. If we serve money in its fallen and corrupted state, entangled within the system of the earth, it will arc with time in its fallen and corrupted state, this gets humanity arcing with both time and money while they both sit under the sun and we end up serving them both. They communicate and arc together and we get paid for how much time we work. If the poverty spirit is present it will be even worse because we'll be working for money and time, just keeping our heads above water not being able to expand as a king in wealth, riches and prosperity because we're bound to the earth. To get away from serving money, time and the poverty spirit, in their fallen and corrupted state, we have to change the way we think.

My knowledge on this subject is being expanded all the time and I want to channel finances to what I'm feeling through the compassion of my heart and my union with Yahweh. I don't just want to hold someone's hand and say a little prayer, because it's the finance that comes from my mountain that establishes something and that supersedes the expectation that they have in their personal life. When we arc with Mammon we have a union which brings about transformation. So many of us are wanting this and are engaging with this and while I've been speaking about this and writing this, a trading floor has opened to bring about a shift within the lives of those wanting to engage fully.

When I was engaging with Mammon and looking into some things I saw something above him, the Beings of Gold, Silver and Copper. They created an arcing which was almost an entanglement of what was unfolding. I had already formed individual relationships with these three Beings prior to this encounter and felt that this all made sense. I began to honour Gold that was in my life, which brings wealth and riches. I began to honour Silver and Silver's function and likewise with Copper. As I looked, I saw Melchizedek seated just above these three Beings. I beheld him in his government and the order of what he carries. There was such a sense of government as I beheld what was happening and an arcing was taking place which brought about a transformation, because of the encounter which had set me on a journey to understand that we are kings and priests who operate from a different realm.

When we begin to engage within this process, they arc together with us and we see the establishment of that through Hunger and Desire, understanding that we have a record which needs to be revealed in creation. When we arc with everything that is happening and we set our feet as a *Vav* or a hook in creation we begin to display the encounters that we have. This has completely changed my perspective on my position as a son, a king and a priest, for me to bring about the transformation that I want to see happen within the area of influence that I walk in. When these Beings begin to arc together with us – which is a big deal to be honest – it gives us the administration to begin to function in a capacity that opens up a trading floor.

Take a moment and this opportunity to trade into this and

arc together with what is taking place with Mammon within your heart. I want you to behold who you are and what is taking place within your arena as a son, as a king and as a priest. By faith, I want you to engage and behold what is taking place. I'm fully aware that Mammon, which is many of – plural, is beginning to engage with my mountain, which in turn is engaging with your mountains to begin to behold something specific that is going to unfold within your life as you've been engaging within this process of maturity. I honour the trading floor right now and I honour the government that Melchizedek carries to administrate together with us. I arc now with Lindi and the House of Masters working together with myself, Elpida Ministries, and all the mountains that are present, and as this trading floor is very evident before us today, we trade into it with the value of a shift that is not going to only change our lives, but it's going to change and set up those who are to come. Those that are beholding the countenance, those that are seated within the Kingdom Realms right now, emanating the truth of who they are and beginning to behold this trade for generations to come. That this will set a mark within families' mountains, to bring about this glorious freedom and liberty that Paul speaks about. We can set in motion what it is to be a king and a priest.

Whatever you are now feeling prompted to do within your relationship with Yahweh, I want you to step out by faith upon this trading platform and I want you to trade with purpose into what is taking place within this arena. I'm going to arc and hold this trading platform with what is taking place as we begin to administrate this. We thank You, Yahweh, for all of the Beings that are beginning to witness this trade. As you put down this trade, they are beholding what is taking place within this arena, witnessing the trade that is bringing about a shift within your life that is going to impact generations to come as you behold this process.

Mammon, I honour the relationship that I have with you and how you have been such a key Being within the administration of wealth and riches from the Treasury Room of Yahweh's Kingdom within my life. As we've been walking within this relationship, I've seen how we've been able to administrate, through the union that I have with Yahweh and a co-labouring relationship arcing together. We are bringing about a significant shift to creation. You have given us a perspective in the truth in engaging with you and engaging with time, in its righteous position that begins to serve us. Mammon, you want to serve us as sons. You want to engage with us as sons. You want to release finances from the Vault of the Treasury Room for us to administrate a transformation here in creation and you are watching how we are stewarding all things. So I just engage over this trading platform right now. I receive what is happening and I arc together to behold the mystery of what is unfolding for us as a Tribe and as a people.

The significance of what just happened is that it transforms our lives and also brings in a legacy for the generations that are still to come so they can reap a reward of a trade that we did and which took place in this moment.

About Lindi

Lindi Masters has been in active ministry for 41 years.
Her heart is to mentor the Body of Yeshua into 'Maturity
being their Vav', rooted and grounded in YHVH and in His
mysteries and secrets.
Lindi has a legacy of 3 incredible children who have
all married Godly partners and she has 4 beautiful
grandchildren.

She currently divides her time between the UK and South
Africa.

About Ricky

Ricky's heart is to challenge and encourage others on how to become Sons of Yahweh. He shares from his Kingdom encounters that have taught him about the importance of being positioned correctly as a Son, how to govern as a Son, journeying with Faith and untangling from the religious spirit.

Ricky is married to Melanie and together they have two children and reside in Durban, South Africa.